Live English Grammar **Elementary**

Contents

Unit 1

Present Simple
Present Progressive

Percy the drummer

Read the text below.

Percy **wakes up** at 9 o'clock every morning. He **doesn't work** in the morning and he usually **stays** at home.

In the evening Percy **goes** to work. He **plays** the drums in an orchestra.

This week Percy **is staying** in Birmingham. His orchestra **is giving** some concerts there. Tonight they'**re playing** at the Symphony Hall.

It's 8 o'clock now and Percy **is running** to the concert hall. He's late!

Percy is finally on stage and he'**s running** to his place, but...

Are the following sentences True or False? Write T or F in the boxes.

1 Percy always stays at home in the morning. ☐
2 Percy works in the evening. ☐
3 Percy is a musician. ☐
4 Percy lives in Birmingham. ☐
5 The orchestra is giving a concert at the Symphony Hall. ☐

Grammar

a Present Simple

We use the **Present Simple**:

- for habitual actions or actions which are repeated in the present.
  I usually wake up at 8 o'clock.
- for permanent states in the present.
  He works in a bank.
- for general truths.
  The moon goes round the Earth.

Time Expressions
always, usually, often, sometimes, rarely, never
every day/morning/week/year, etc.
once/twice/three times, etc. a week/day, etc.
on Fridays, in spring, in the afternoon, etc.

Affirmative	Negative	
	FULL FORMS	SHORT FORMS
I read	I do not read	I don't read
He/She/It reads	He/She/It does not read	He/She/It doesn't read
We/You/They read	We/You/They do not read	We/You/They don't read

Interrogative	Short Answers	
Do I read?	Yes, I do.	No, I don't.
Does he/she/it read?	Yes, he/she/it does.	No, he/she/it doesn't.
Do we/you/they read?	Yes, we/you/they do.	No, we/you/they don't.

Spelling

I watch → he watches
I fish → he fishes
I pass → she passes
I fix → she fixes
I go → it goes
I study → he studies **but** I play → she plays

Note: The **frequency adverbs always**, **usually**, **often**, **sometimes**, **rarely**, **never** usually go before the **main verb**, but after the verb ***be***.

He always goes to school by bus.
He doesn't always go to school by bus.
Does he always go to school by bus?
She is always late.

b Present Progressive

We use the **Present Progressive**:

- for actions that are happening now, at the moment of speaking.
  Look! A boy is running across the street.
- to describe temporary situations or actions that are happening at present, but not necessarily at the moment of speaking.
  She's working in a supermarket these days.
- for actions that we have planned to do in the near future (we usually mention when).
  Peter is leaving for Paris next week.

Time Expressions
now, right now, at the moment
at present, these days, today
this week/year, etc.
tonight, tomorrow, on Wednesday, etc.
next week/year, etc.

Affirmative		Negative	
FULL FORMS	SHORT FORMS	FULL FORMS	SHORT FORMS
I am reading	I'm reading	I am not reading	I'm not reading
He/She/It is reading	He/She/It's reading	He/She/It is not reading	He/She/It isn't reading
We/You/They are reading	We/You/They're reading	We/You/They are not reading	We/You/They aren't reading

Interrogative	Short Answers	
Am I reading?	Yes, I am.	No, I'm not.
Is he/she/it reading?	Yes, he/she/it is.	No, he/she/it isn't.
Are we/you/they reading?	Yes, we/you/they are.	No, we/you/they aren't.

Spelling

come → coming
cut → cutting
begin → beginning
lie → lying
travel → travelling

but

agree → agreeing
eat → eating
visit → visiting
study → studying
sail → sailing

Note: Certain verbs are usually **not** used in the **Present Progressive**. These verbs are called **stative verbs** and usually express:

- **senses**: smell, taste, hear, etc.
- **emotions**: love, like, hate, want, etc.
- **thought**, **knowledge**, **belief**: know, think, understand, etc.
- various other **states**, such as: cost, own, seem, appear, etc.

activities

a Look the prompts. Write questions and answers, as in the example.

1 Sandra / speak / German / ?
→ No / English and French

Does Sandra speak German?
No, she doesn't. She speaks English and French.

2 frogs / live / near lakes / ?
→ Yes

____
____

3 Jennifer / go / work / car / ?
→ No / train

____
____

4 zebras / live / Africa / ?
→ Yes

____
____

5 lions / eat / leaves / ?
→ No / meat

____
____

6 Mr Andrews /teach /maths /?
→ No / geography

____
____

b **Look at the pictures and the prompts. Write questions and answers, as in the example.**

1 Debbie / run / ?

Is Debbie running?

No, she isn't. She's walking.

2 Debbie / smile / ?

3 Debbie / carry / umbrella / ?

4 Julie and Peter / stand / ?

5 Julie and Peter / listen / music / ?

6 Julie / wear / trousers / ?

7 they / sit / at / table / ?

8 they / watch / TV / ?

9 they / drink / milk / ?

c **Complete the sentences with the Present Simple or the Present Progressive of the verbs in brackets.**

1 ____*Do*____ Stephen and Jack ____*always play*____ (always / play) basketball in the afternoon?

2 Daniel ________ (fly) to Rome tomorrow morning.

3 Wendy is at home. She ________ (watch) TV.

4 ________ Sheila ________ (know) Mrs Jones?

5 John and Mary ________ (learn) Italian this year.

6 ________ Angie ________ (often / cook) chicken for dinner?

7 ________ we ________ (go) to the cinema this Saturday?

8 I ________ (not understand) this exercise!

9 Jenny ________ (walk) to school every day. She ________ (never / take) the bus.

10 Ann and Jane ________ (not want) to watch the football match because they ________ (not like) football.

d **Look at the pictures and write sentences, as in the example. Use the Present Simple and the Present Progressive of the verbs in the box.**

listen	play	~~write~~	sleep	~~take~~	climb	fly	make	talk	study

SUNDAY MORNING

usually

now

1 Mr Smith *usually writes letters on Sunday morning but now he's taking pictures.*
____

2 Mrs Smith ______________________________
____
____

3 Tony ______________________________
____
____

4 Melissa ______________________________
____
____

5 The cats ______________________________
____
____

e **Complete the texts with the Present Simple or the Present Progressive of the verbs in the boxes.**

~~have~~	have	have	cook	dance	invite	play	make

1 Every year Helen (**1**) ___*has*___ a party on her birthday. Her mother (**2**) ______________ a lot of food and (**3**) ______________ a big cake. Helen (**4**) ______________ all her friends and classmates. They (**5**) ______________ , (**6**) ______________ games and (**7**) ______________ lots of fun. This year Helen (**8**) ______________ the party next Saturday afternoon.

stay	travel	return	meet	fly

2 Mr Foster often (**9**) ______________ abroad on business. Tomorrow he (**10**) ______________ to Germany. He (**11**) ______________ there for three days and he (**12**) ______________ some German businessmen. He (**13**) ______________ to London on Thursday evening.

not want	think	go	take	not like

3 Emma (**14**) ______________ to work by bus every morning. Today she (**15**) ______________ a taxi because she (**16**) ______________ to be late. However, she (**17**) ______________ taxis because she (**18**) ______________ they are expensive.

f Communication

Work in pairs.

Student A Go to page 136

Student B Go to page 144

vocabulary box

watch cartoons
clean room
wash car
have coffee with friend
skate with friends
go on picnic
go shopping
work in garden

g *writing*

Imagine you are on a camping holiday near a beach. Write a postcard to a friend, telling him/her what you do every day and what you are doing today. Use the ideas given and your own.

get up
have lunch / dinner
have a good time
swim
lie on beach
sunbathe
play sports
do water sports
cook over a fire

....
....
....
....
....
....
....
....

Unit 2

Articles
Nouns

Dublin Bus Ride

Read the text. Complete the blanks with a, an, the or –.

Welcome to Dublin Bus Ride, ladies and gentlemen... We're now passing **the** Gate Theatre and turning into O' Connell Street, one of **the** widest streets in _____ world. Ahead of us is **the** River Liffey. We're now crossing O' Connell Bridge and going towards Trinity College. Trinity College is _____ oldest university in _____ Ireland.

And now we are turning into _____ Dame Street and we're going to see **a** beautiful old building, Dublin Castle. After that, we're going to visit _____ old church, Christ Church Cathedral. Finally, we're going to have _____ lunch at _____ traditional Irish pub.

River Liffey

Trinity College

Christ Church Cathedral

Grammar

a Articles

The Indefinite Article *a/an*

- We use the **indefinite article *a/an*** before singular countable nouns.
  a pen *an apple*

We use **a/an**:

- When we speak about something that is not specific. *There's a man at the door.*
- for professions. *She's a teacher.*

The Definite Article *the*

- We use the **definite article *the*** before uncountable nouns and before countable nouns, both in the singular and in the plural.
  the milk *the pen* *the pens*

We use **the** before:

- something **specific** or **unique**.
  The man at the door is my uncle. *The sun rises in the east.*
- names of **seas**, **oceans**, **rivers**, **deserts**.
  the Mediterranean (Sea) *the Atlantic (Ocean)* *the Amazon (River)* *the Sahara (Desert)*
- **groups of islands**, **mountain ranges**, and **countries** in the **plural**.
  the Canary Islands *the Himalayas* *the USA*
- people's **surnames** (when we refer to the whole family).
  the Smiths
- **nationalities** (when we refer to the whole nation).
  the Greeks **but** *Fiona is Italian.*
- **musical instruments** (with the verb *play*).
  He plays the piano.
- names of **hotels**, **cinemas**, **newspapers**.
  the Hilton Hotel *the Rex Cinema* *the Times*
- the **cardinal points**.
  in the east
- the **superlative** form of adjectives and adverbs.
  Tom is the tallest boy in this class.

We **do not** use **the** before:

- names of **people**, **cities**, **islands**, **lakes**, **countries**, **streets**, **continents**, **nationalities**.
  That's Maria. She comes from Spain.
- School **subjects** or **sports**.
  History is interesting. *We love football.*
- Uncountable nouns and plural countable nouns, when we talk about something in **general**.
  I like coffee. *Cats like milk.*
- The words **breakfast**, **lunch**, **dinner**.
  We have lunch at 1:30.
- The words **hospital**, **home**, **school**, **church**, **bed**, **work**, **prison**, when they are used for the purpose for which they exist.
  The boys are at school. **but** *The boys visited their uncle at the hospital.*

b Nouns

Nouns refer to people, animals, things, material, situations, states, etc. They can be **countable** or **uncountable**.

Countable Nouns

Countable nouns can be counted. They have singular and plural forms. We can use **a/an** before them in the singular and **numbers** in the plural.

Plural Form

pen → pens
box → boxes
watch → watches
brush → brushes
tomato → tomatoes **but** piano → pianos, radio → radios
baby → babies **but** toy → toys
knife → knives
leaf → leaves **but** roof → roofs

Irregular Nouns	
man → men	mouse → mice
woman → women	person → people
child → children	sheep → sheep
foot → feet	fish → fish
tooth → teeth	deer → deer
goose → geese	

Uncountable Nouns

Uncountable nouns cannot be counted. They only have singular form. We cannot use **a/an** or **numbers** before them.

milk *water* *butter* *wood* *glass* *money* *time*

Note: To define the quantity of uncountable nouns we can use words such as: **bottle**, **piece**, **loaf, slice**, **carton**, **cup**, **glass**, **packet**, **kilo**, **litre**, **box**, **bar**, **bowl**, etc. before them.
a carton of milk *a loaf/slice of bread*

activities

a Complete the sentences with a, an, the or -.

1 *The* Guardian is *a* newspaper.
2 ___ my grandfather is ___ old man.
3 ___ duck is ___ bird.
4 ___ pink is ___ beautiful colour.
5 ___ Smiths are staying at ___ Carlton Hotel.
6 ___ Earth is ___ planet.
7 *Mary Poppins* is on at ___ Odeon Cinema.
8 ___ Ann is in ___ bed because she's ill.

b Complete the blanks with the or -.

(**1**) *The* USA is a big country in (**2**) _____ North America. (**3**) _____ Canada is to (**4**) _____ north of this country and (**5**) _____ Mexico is to (**6**) _____ south. To (**7**) _____ east of (**8**) _____ country lies (**9**) _____ Atlantic Ocean and to (**10**) _____ west (**11**) _____ Pacific Ocean. There are a lot of mountains and two big mountain ranges, (**12**) _____ Appalachian Mountains in (**13**) _____ east and (**14**) _____ Rocky Mountains in (**15**) _____ west. There are about (**16**) _____ twenty big rivers in (**17**) _____ country. (**18**) _____ longest river is (**19**) _____ Mississipi - Missouri. In (**20**) _____ north there are five big lakes. (**21**) _____ largest lake is (**22**) _____ Lake Superior. There are also two deserts in (**23**) _____ USA, (**24**) _____ Colorado Desert and (**25**) _____ Mojave Desert.

c **This is Donna's souvenir shopping list. Look at the pictures and complete the blanks.**

1 Two _watches_  for the twins.

2 ____________  for Ed and Carl.

3 Some ____________  for aunt Emma.

4 Two ____________  of biscuits for Pam.

5 Kitchen ____________  for mum.

6 Two hair ____________  for Tina.

7 ____________  for Danny and Peter.

8 ____________  for the baby.

9 English ____________  for Claire and Ingrid.

10 Two ____________  for dad.

d **Read the texts below. Complete the blanks with a, an , the or -.**

1 (**1**) ______ Jeanette is (**2**) ______ French. She lives in (**3**) ______ village in (**4**) ______ France. (**5**) ______ village is near (**6**) ______ Paris, so she often goes there. (**7**) ______ Jeanette lives in (**8**) ______ yellow house in (**9**) ______ centre of (**10**) ______ village. (**11**) ______ house has got (**12**) ______ living room, (**13**) ______ two bedrooms, (**14**) ______ kitchen and (**15**) ______ bathroom. There is also (**16**) ______ big studio. (**17**) ______ Jeanette works there. She's (**18**) ______ artist. She paints (**19**) ______ pictures. In front of (**20**) ______ house there is (**21**) ______ big garden. There are (**22**) ______ flowers, (**23**) ______ apple tree, (**24**) ______ vegetable garden and (**25**) ______ dog-house in (**26**) ______ garden. (**27**) ______ Jeanette's dog, (**28**) ______ Rex, sleeps in (**29**) ______ dog-house.

2 (**30**) ______ Dennis is my best friend. He's (**31**) ______ student. He lives on (**32**) ______ Prince Street. Every day he wakes up, has (**33**) ______ breakfast and goes to (**34**) ______ school. He likes school and wants to become (**35**) ______ teacher. After school he has (**36**) ______ guitar lesson. He likes (**37**) ______ music very much and he plays (**38**) ______ guitar very well. He has got (**39**) ______ old guitar. It was (**40**) ______ present from his grandfather.

e Look at the picture below and write what's on the table.

1 *Two bowls of* cornflakes.
2 ______________ cheese.
3 ______________ water.
4 ______________ bread.
5 ______________ cake.
6 ______________ milk.
7 ______________ biscuits.
8 ______________ sugar.
9 ______________ chocolate.
10 ______________ sweets.
11 ______________ tea.
12 ______________ orange juice.

f can you remember?

Read Julie's project about her town and circle the correct words.

My town

I **live** / **lives** in **the** / **–** Clinwood. **The** / **–** Clinwood is **a** / **the** small town in **–** / **the** USA. My town has got **a** / **an** hospital, two **church** / **churches**, two **school** / **schools**, **the** / **a** nice park, **a** / **an** old train station and **a** / **–** cinema.

I **am liking** / **like** my town because it is nice and quiet. On weekdays I **am going** / **go** to **–** / **the** school. At weekends I **stay** / **am staying** at home or I **am going** / **go** out with my friends.

This is **a** / **an** picture of **the** / **–** park. I **ride** / **am riding** my horse and my friend Lisa **looks** / **is looking** at me.

g Communication

Work in pairs. How much do you know? Look at the prompts below, ask questions and discuss with your partner, as in the example. Then, check your answers.

vocabulary box

desert
canyon
mountain range

1. Amazon River → Venezuela / Brazil
2. Grand Canyon → USA / Mexico
3. Canberra → Australia / New Zealand
4. Gobi Desert → Asia / Africa
5. Andes → group of islands / mountain range
6. Lake Winnipeg → USA / Canada
7. Galapagos Islands → Pacific Ocean / Mediterranean Sea
8. Mount Kilimanjaro → South Africa / Kenya

e.g. **A :** *Is the Amazon River in Venezuela?*
B : *Yes, I think so. / No, I don't think so. I think it's in Brazil.*

Answers

1. The Amazon River is in Brazil.
2. The Grand Canyon is in the USA.
3. Canberra is in Australia.
4. The Gobi Desert is in Asia.
5. The Andes are a mountain range.
6. Lake Winnipeg is in Canada.
7. The Galapagos Islands are in the Pacific Ocean.
8. Mount Kilimanjaro is in Kenya.

h writing

What do you usually have for breakfast? What's your ideal breakfast? Write a few sentences using the words in the boxes.

glass cup bowl
slice piece

milk egg cake
bread cheese
ham banana
apple orange juice
toast cornflakes

....
....
....
....
....
....
....
....

Unit 3

Some / Any / No / Every
Much / Many / A lot of
A few / A little
How much? / How many?

How much do you know about the koala?

Read the text below.

A lot of people think that the koala is a kind of bear, but it isn't. The koala is a marsupial. This means that it has a special pocket on its belly. The koala mother uses it to carry her babies **everywhere**.

The koala is an amazing animal. It doesn't eat **anything** except eucalyptus leaves and it drinks **no** water. It needs only **a little** water and it gets it from the eucalyptus leaves.

The koala moves slowly and needs **a lot of** sleep. **How many** hours does the koala sleep **every** day? About twenty-two!

Which of the facts below are true about the koala? Tick the correct boxes.

1 The koala is not a bear. ☐
2 The koala carries its babies in a special pocket. ☐
3 The koala eats **lots of** different things. ☐
4 The koala doesn't drink **any** water. ☐
5 The koala runs very fast. ☐
6 The koala sleeps only **a few** hours **every** day. ☐

Grammar

a Some / Any / No / Every and their compounds

Some, **any** and **no** are used with uncountable nouns or with plural countable nouns.

- **Some** is used in affirmative sentences and in questions when we offer something or when we ask for something politely.
  There's some coffee on the table. Would you like some milk? Can I have some water?
- **Any** is used in questions and in negative sentences.
  Are there any books on the desk? There aren't any books on the desk.
- **No** is used in affirmative sentences, but it has a negative meaning (= not any).
  There's no milk in the glass. = There isn't any milk in the glass.
- **Every** is used with singular countable nouns.
  Every student has got a bag.

Note: **Some** and **any** can also be used as pronouns. In this case, they are not followed by a noun.
Is there any orange juice in the bottle? No, there isn't any.

Compounds of:	SOME	ANY	NO	EVERY
People	someone somebody	anyone anybody	no one nobody	everyone everybody
Things	something	anything	nothing	everything
Places	somewhere	anywhere	nowhere	everywhere

The **compounds** of **some, any**, **no** and **every** are used in the same way as **some, any**, **no** and **every**, but they are not followed by a noun. The verb in the sentence is always singular.

b Much / Many / A lot of / A little / A few

- **Much** and **a little** are used before uncountable nouns.
  There isn't much sugar in the bowl. There's a little sugar in the bowl.
- **Many** and **a few** are used before plural countable nouns.
  Are there many chairs in the room? There are a few chairs in the room.
- **A lot of** is used before uncountable nouns and plural countable nouns.
  There's a lot of sugar in the bowl. There are a lot of chairs in the room.

We use:

- **Much** only in questions and in negative sentences.
- **Many** usually in questions and in negative sentences.
- **A lot of**, **a little**, **a few** in affirmative sentences.

Notes:
- **Much**, **many**, **a few**, **a little** can be used as pronouns. In this case, they are not followed by a noun.
  How much money have you got? I haven't got much.
  Are there many eggs in the fridge? No, only a few.
- When we speak, we can use **lots of** instead of **a lot of**. The corresponding pronouns are **lots** and **a lot**.
  There are lots of pens on my desk. There are a lot.

c How much? / How many?

- **How much + uncountable noun**: we ask about quantity. *How much milk is there in the fridge?*
- **How many + countable noun**: we ask about number. *How many books have we got?*
- **How much is ...?** : to ask about the price of something. *How much is this shirt?*

activities

a Choose *a*, *b* or *c*.

1 There aren't ___*any*___ books in my bag.
a. some (b.) any c. no

2 Would you like __________ milk in your coffee?
a. some b. every c. no

3 Mrs Smith helps __________ student in the class.
a. some b. any c. every

4 James is very good at his job and has __________ problems at work.
a. any b. no c. every

5 Does Kate speak __________ foreign languages?
a. any b. no c. some

6 I'm going to the cinema with __________ friends. Are you coming?
a. no b. every c. some

7 __________ child likes cartoons.
a. Every b. Some c. Everybody

8 There is __________ water in the fridge.
a. any b. every c. no

9 The twins didn't drink __________ tea because they didn't like it.
a. some b. any c. every

10 There are __________ CDs on the desk.
a. every b. any c. some

b Read the dialogues. Complete the blanks in the sentences with compounds of some, any, no and every.

1 **Alex:** Do you know where the cat is?
Mary: No, I can't find her ___*anywhere*___.
Alex: Well, she's __________ in the house. Look again!
Mary: I looked __________ and the cat is __________ .

2 **Shop assistant:** Would you like __________ else?
Becky: No, I don't need __________ else. I think I've got __________ .
Oh, wait! Yes, I need __________ else, too. I need a few pencils.

3 **Teacher:** OK __________ , quiet please. Now, can __________ answer the question?
Kevin: Miss, I think there is __________ outside.
Teacher: What? Let's see. No, there is __________ there. Now, back to our question...

c Look at Tina's room and write what she has got. Use **much**, **many**, and **a lot of** / **lots of**, as in the example.

1 She *hasn't got many* CDs.
2 She ______________ money.
3 She ______________ books.
4 She ______________ posters.
5 She ______________ homework.
6 She ______________ orange juice.
7 She ______________ bags.
8 She ______________ photographs.

d Read the dialogues. Complete the blanks with **how much**, **how many**, **a little**, **a few**.

1
Michelle: Have you got any sugar and eggs?
Anita: Yes, I've got *a little* sugar and ______________ eggs.
Michelle: Well, can you give me some?
Anita: Of course. ______________ sugar do you want?
Michelle: Oh, one cup, please.
Anita: OK, and ______________ eggs do you need?
Michelle: Three, please. Thank you.

2
Johnny: Mum, I'm hungry. Is there anything in the fridge?
Mother: Yes, there are ______________ sandwiches and there is ______________ orange juice.

3
Alicia: Hi, Jane, it's Alicia. ______________ homework have you got today?
Jane: Just ______________. What about you?
Alicia: Well, I've only got ______________ maths problems. Let's meet in an hour and go to the park.

e ## can you remember?

Read the text and circle the correct words.

(**1**) (–) / **The** Mr and Mrs Simpson are at (**2**) **the** / **a** restaurant. There are only (**3**) **a few** / **a little** people in (**4**) **the** / **a** restaurant. (**5**) **The** / – Simpsons are sitting at (**6**) – / **a** table near (**7**) **-** / **the** window. There is (**8**) **an** / **a** orange vase with (**9**) **a** / **some** flowers in it on (**10**) **a** / **the** table. There is (**11**) **a** / **the** candle near (**12**) **a** / **the** vase. At the moment (**13**) **the** / **-** Simpsons aren't eating (**14**) **no / any** food. (**15**) **The / -** Mr Simpson is drinking (**16**) **a / some** coffee. (**17**) **The / -** Mrs Simpson has got (**18**) **a / some** glass of lemonade in front of her but she isn't drinking it because she doesn't like it. She wants (**19**) **some / much** water but there isn't (**20**) **much / many** in (**21**) **a / the** bottle on their table.

f Communication

Work in pairs. Ask your partner questions about himself / herself. Then answer your partner's questions. Use *much, many, a lot of, a few, a little, no, any* and ideas from the vocabulary box.

vocabulary box

posters / there / be / your room	money / have / pocket / now
books / usually / borrow / library	free time / have / weekends
computer games / have	milk / drink / every day
puzzles / have	fruit / eat / every day

e.g. **A :** *How many posters are there in your room?*
B : *There are a lot of / a few / no posters in my room.*

g writing

What's in your bedroom? Write a few sentences. Use some, any, no, much, many, a lot of, a little, a few and the ideas in the box.

book	photograph
poster	magazine
CD	painting
clothes	toy
plant	

....
....
....
....
....
....
....
....
....
....
....
....
....

Unit 4

Object Personal Pronouns
Possessive Adjectives
Possessive Pronouns
Possessive Case

What's in a name?

Read the text below.

John Wayne

You don't like **your** name? Well, you can always change **it**[1]. These famous people changed **theirs** a long time ago...

- John Wayne was a famous American actor. **His**[2] real name was Marion Morrison.
- Elton John is a famous British singer. What is **Elton John's** real name? Reginald Dwight.

Elton John

Did you know...?

- The king **of Portugal** Alfonso II lived at the beginning **of the 13th century**. People called **him**[3] 'Alfonso the Fat'. Can you guess why?
- The Swedish pop group ABBA got **its**[4] name from **its members'** first names. **Their** names were Agnetha, Benny, Bjorn and Annifried.

ABBA

Mel B

Famous people sometimes give **their** children strange names...

- Mel B, a member **of the group** *The Spice Girls*, calls **her**[5] daughter Phoenix Chi.
- Bob Geldof is a singer, too. **His children's** names are Fifi Trixibelle, Pixie and Peaches!

What do these words refer to? Look at the numbered words in the text.

1 it ______________

2 His ______________

3 him ______________

4 its ______________

5 her ______________

Now answer these questions.

6 Who's Phoenix Chi's mother?

____

7 Whose daughter is called Peaches?

____

Grammar

a Object Personal Pronouns, Possessive Adjectives, Possessive Pronouns

Subject Personal Pronouns	Object Personal Pronouns	Possessive Adjectives	Possessive Pronouns
I	me	my	mine
you	you	your	yours
he	him	his	his
she	her	her	hers
it	it	its	——
we	us	our	ours
you	you	your	yours
they	them	their	theirs

Object personal pronouns are used after verbs as objects or after prepositions.

We saw them at the cinema. Is he talking to you?

Possessive adjectives

- They always go before nouns and they don't take articles before them.
  Your house is big.
- They have the same gender and number as the possessors.
  She is a student. Her desk is here.
  They are teachers. Their books are on the desk.

Possessive pronouns are used instead of **possessive adjective + noun,** so they are never followed by a noun.

That's her pet. ➔ *That's hers.*

b Possessive Case ('s)

The **possessive case** shows that something belongs to someone (person or animal).

This is Mary's car. The cat's eyes are blue.

We form the **possessive case**:

- **Singular nouns** take **'s** (apostrophe + s).
  This is the girl's T-shirt.
- **Regular plural** nouns take **'** (only apostrophe).
  The babies' hands are small.
- **Irregular plural** nouns take **'s** (apostrophe + s).
  The women's dresses are short.
- Proper nouns which end in **-s** take **'s** or **'** (apostrophe + s or only apostrophe).
  This is James's ***or*** *James' house.*

Notes:

- When two or more possessors own the same thing, we add the **possessive case** only to the last noun.
  Mike and Helen's car is new. (Mike and Helen own the same car.)
- When two or more possessors own two or more different things, we add the **possessive case** to each possessor.
  Mike's and Helen's cars are new. (Mike and Helen own different cars.)

- We omit the noun that follows the **possessive case** when we have already mentioned it, when it is easy to understand or when it refers to a place.
  That's not your book. It's Judy's (book). *Where are you going? To the newsagent's.*
- We can answer questions with **whose** using possessive pronouns or the possessive case.
  Whose is this pen? It's mine. *Whose box is this? It's Diana's.*

of + noun

We use **of + noun** to show that something belongs to a thing (inanimate) or to an abstract noun.
Do you like the colour of this T-shirt? *The front door of the house was open all night.*

activities

a Complete the sentences. Use possessive adjectives or possessive pronouns.

1 John has got a bicycle. ___*His*___ bicycle is green. That red bicycle isn't ___*his*___ .

2 Mary has got a watch. __________ watch is black. That brown watch isn't ______ .

3 Alan and Mark have got a dog. __________ dog is white. That black dog isn't _______ .

4 We have got a car. __________ car is yellow. That blue car isn't ______ .

5 I have got a lamp. _________ lamp is orange. That green lamp isn't _______ .

6 My brother has got a guitar. ______ guitar is red. That brown guitar isn't ________ .

b Complete the dialogues with subject personal pronouns, object personal pronouns, possessive adjectives or possessive pronouns.

1 **Emily:** Dad, can (**1**) ___*you*___ help (**2**) Tom and ________ with (**3**) ________ homework?
Dad: What's the problem?
Emily: (**4**) ________ don't understand (**5**) ________ chemistry homework and I must finish (**6**) ______ today. Tom needs help with (**7**) ________ , too.
Dad: OK, I think I can help (**8**) _______ both with (**9**) _______ homework.

2 **Kevin:** Are these sunglasses (**10**) ________ , Marta?
Marta: No, (**11**) ________ aren't. They're Tina's. Give (**12**) ________ to (**13**) ________ .
Kevin: Hey Tina, take (**14**) ________ sunglasses.

Tina: They aren't (**15**) ________ . (**16**) ________ sunglasses are at home. I think they're Betty's. Yes, I'm sure, they're (**17**) ________ .

3 Susan: Where are (**18**) ________ parents? (**19**) ________ car isn't in the garage.
Linda: They're shopping for the dinner party tomorrow evening. You see, (**20**) ________ cousin Ralph from the USA is visiting (**21**) ________ tomorrow.
Susan: Really? Can I come too? I want to meet (**22**) ________ .
Linda: Sure. Why not? And (**23**) ________ can all go out after dinner.

4 Tony: Girls, is that dog (**24**) ________?
Anne: No, it isn't (**25**) ________ . (**26**) ________ ears are brown, our dog has got white ears.
Tony: Is it Mary's then?
Kate: No, it isn't (**27**) ________ . (**28**) ________ hasn't got a dog.

c Join the sentences below using the possessive case or of + noun.

1 Patty has got two brothers. They're tall.
Patty's brothers are tall.

2 The boys have got jackets. They're dirty.
____

3 The children have got a ball. It's in a tree.
____

4 My blue dress has got buttons. They're yellow.
____

5 Anna and Helen have got a piano. It's black.
____

6 Keith has got a bag and Samantha has got a bag. They're new.
____

7 The team has got a captain. He's young.
____

d Read the sentences, look at the pictures and write where the people are, as in the example.

1 Sally wants a newspaper.
She's at the newsagent's.

2 Mark wants some carrots and oranges.
____

3 Stella wants some bread.

____

4 Samuel wants some meat.

____

e can you remember?

Circle the correct words.

Mark is (**1**) **me** / **my** best friend. (**2**) **We** / **Us** do (**3**) **much** / **lots of** things together. (**4**) **Mark's** / **Marks'** house is near (**5**) **my** / **mine**. It's a big house with a big garden. There are (**6**) **a little** / **a few** trees in the garden. There's (**7**) **something** / **anything** special about one of the trees: Mark has got a treehouse in (**8**) **its** / **it**. (**9**) **We** / **Our** spend (**10**) **many** / **a lot of** time there because it's (**11**) **our** / **ours** favourite place. We usually go there (**12**) **every** / **any** afternoon and do (**13**) **us** / **our** homework. We sit and work on the floor because there aren't (**14**) **no** / **any** chairs or tables in the treehouse. On Wednesdays we don't have (**15**) **much** / **a lot** homework so we go there and play board games. My two brothers love the treehouse too and we sometimes invite (**16**) **their** / **them** to come. At the weekend we go to the treehouse and listen to music. I've got (**17**) **a lot of** / **much** CDs but Mark hasn't got (**18**) **any** / **some**, so I bring (**19**) **my** / **mine**. Mark and I have great fun together and I like (**20**) **him** / **his** very much.

f Communication

Work in pairs.

Student A Go to page 137

Student B Go to page 145

vocabulary box

greengrocer's
baker's
hairdresser's
butcher's
newsagent's
chemist's

g writing

Write a paragraph about your best friend as in exercise *e*. Answer the following questions.

Who is your best friend?
Where does he/she live?
How do you spend your time together?
Why do you like him/her?

....

....

....

....

....

....

Unit 5

Adjectives
Adverbs
Comparisons

Second-hand cars

Steve wants to buy a second-hand car. Yesterday he saw four cars and made some notes about them. Read Steve's notes. Which car do you think he will buy?

A

£2,400

This is the biggest of the four cars, but it's the oldest and the noisiest. It's also more difficult to drive in the city than cars B and C.

B

£1,900

This is the cheapest of the cars I saw and it's also the smallest, so you can park it more easily than the others. It is not as old as car A, but it is older than the other two.

C

£2,400

This car is more expensive than car B, but it's more comfortable for long trips. It's as expensive as car A, but it's more modern and easier to drive.

D

£20,000

This is the car of my dreams! It's the fastest and the most modern of all, but it's also the most expensive! I haven't got that much money!...

Complete the sentences with the words in the box.

the cheapest	bigger	older	the most expensive	more easily	more expensive

1 Car B is ____________________ than cars C and D.

2 Car C is ____________________ and ____________________ than car B.

3 Car B is ____________________ of the four cars.

4 Car D is ____________________ of the four cars.

5 You can park car B ____________________ than car A.

Grammar

a Adjectives

Adjectives define nouns. They come before nouns in a sentence and they have no plural form. When they are not followed by a noun, they don't take an article before them.

She's a beautiful girl. *Dogs are clever.* *This bike is green.*

b Adverbs

There are four main categories of adverbs:

- **Adverbs of place**, which define place, usually answer questions beginning with **where**.
  *Where are you going? We're going **out**.*
- **Adverbs of time**, which define time, usually answer questions beginning with **when**.
  *When are you going to Rome? I'm going to Rome **tomorrow**.*
- **Adverbs of frequency**, which describe how often something happens, usually answer questions beginning with **how often**.
  *How often do you play football? I **never** play football.*
- **Adverbs of manner**, which describe the way in which something happens, usually answer questions beginning with **how**.
  *How does she speak? She speaks **loudly**.*

Formation of **adverbs of manner**:

We form most adverbs of manner by adding the ending **-ly** to the corresponding adjective.
nice → nicely

Spelling

easy → easily
terrible → terribly
careful → carefully

Irregular Adverbs

ADJECTIVES	ADVERBS
good	well
fast	fast
hard	hard
early	early
late	late

c Comparisons (Comparative - Superlative Form)

- We use the **comparative form** of adjectives and adverbs to compare two people, animals or things. Adjectives and adverbs in the comparative form are usually followed by **than**.
  The aeroplane is faster than the car. *Jeff runs faster than Tom.*
- We use the **superlative form** of adjectives and adverbs to compare one person, animal or thing with others of the same kind. Adjectives and adverbs in the superlative form always take the definite article **the** and are usually followed by the prepositions **of** or **in**.
  The giraffe is the tallest animal in the world.

Formation of the **Comparative** and the **Superlative Form**

- All one-syllable and most two-syllable adjectives take the endings **-er** in the comparative form and **-est** in the superlative form.
  tall → taller → tallest *fat → fatter → fattest* *happy → happier → happiest*
- We form the comparative of adjectives with three or more syllables (and some two-syllable adjectives) with **more + adjective** and the superlative with **most + adjective**.
  beautiful - more beautiful - most beautiful
- All one-syllable adverbs and early take the endings **-er** in the comparative form and **-est** in the superlative form.
  fast → faster → fastest *early → earlier → earliest*
- We form the comparative of adverbs with three or more syllables with **more + adverb** and the superlative with **most + adverb**.
  nicely → more nicely → most nicely

Irregular Comparatives and Superlatives		
POSITIVE FORM	COMPARATIVE FORM	SUPERLATIVE FORM
good/well	better	best
bad/badly	worse	worst
little	less	least
many/much	more	most
far	farther/further	farthest/furthest

Other Ways of Comparison

- **less + adjective/adverb + than**
  She's less beautiful than her sister. *He drives less carefully than Carl.*
- **the least + adjective/adverb + of/in**
  It's the least expensive restaurant in town.
- **as + adjective/adverb + as**
  She's as clever as her brother. *He drives as carefully as his brother.*
- **not as/so + adjective/adverb + as**
  She's not as/so clever as her brother. *He doesn't drive as/so carefully as his brother.*

activities

a **Complete the sentences below. Use the adjectives in brackets and adverbs that you can form from these adjectives.**

1 Dennis is very ____*quiet*____ . He always does his homework ____*quietly*____ . (quiet)
2 Ann always drives ________ . She's a ________ driver. (careful)
3 Karen and Ben can draw very ________ . They are ________ artists. (good)
4 Mark is a ________ dancer. He dances ________ . (terrible)
5 Diane and Harry are a ________ couple. They live ________ together. (happy)
6 John learnt the poem ________ . He is a ________ learner. (fast)

b **Complete the sentences with the comparative or superlative form of the adverbs in brackets.**

1 Pam cooks ____*better*____ (well) than her sister.
2 Children learn foreign languages ________ (easily) than adults.
3 George plays the piano ________ (badly) than Robin.
4 Alison likes volleyball ________ (much) than basketball, but she likes hockey the ________ (much).
5 Fay wakes up ________ (early) than Elsa, but Carol wakes up the ________ (early) of all.
6 Robert can run ________ (fast) than Philip, but David can run the ________ (fast) of all.
7 Linda paints ________ (beautifully) than Susan, but Debbie paints the ________ (beautifully) of all the students in the class.

c Look at the pictures and the prompts and write sentences. Use as...as and not as/so...as.

1 Andy: 1.78 m, 72 kg

Peter: 1.78 m, 69 kg

tall: *Andy is as tall as Peter.*

thin: *Andy isn't as/so thin as Peter.*

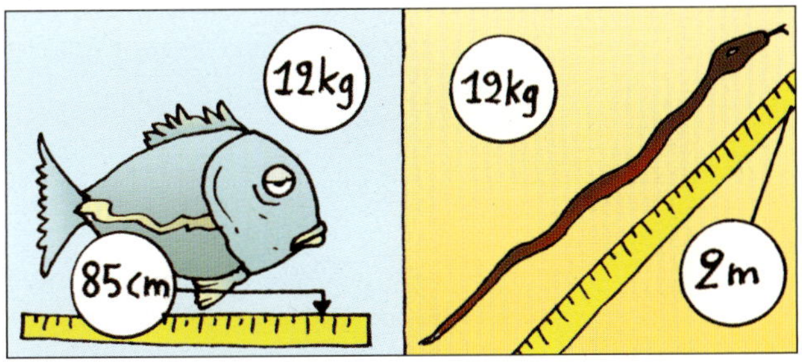

2 fish: 85 cm, 12 kg

snake: 200 cm, 12 kg

long: ______________________

heavy: ______________________

3 Big Wave Hotel: 5,000 tourists a year, 1 km from beach

Fairview Hotel: 5,000 tourists a year, 2 km from beach

popular: ______________________

____

far: ______________________

____

4 museum: 2,000 m^2, built in 1958

bank: 3,500 m^2, built in 1958

big: ______________________

____

old: ______________________

____

d Choose *a*, *b* or *c*.

1 Luke is more polite *than* John.

a. from (**b.**) than c. that

2 History is boring. It is the __________ interesting subject of all.

a. least **b.** most **c.** less

3 Keith doesn't work as __________ as Susan.

a. harder **b.** hardest **c.** hard

4 Sarah dances __________ beautifully as Amy.

a. as **b.** not as **c.** so

5 Dan writes less __________ than Will.

a. nice **b.** nicely **c.** nicer

e Look at the pictures and the prompts and write sentences. Use the comparative and superlative forms of the adjectives given.

fast - slow

1 train / plane

The train is slower than the plane.

2 car / three

The car is the slowest of the three.

3 plane / car

______

heavy - light

7 chair / sofa

______

8 sofa / three

______

9 armchair / chair

______

tall - short

4 Ron / all

______

5 Fay / Susan

______

6 Susan / three

______

expensive - cheap

10 jacket / T-shirt

______

11 jacket / three

______

12 gloves / T-shirt

______

f ## can you remember?

There are two mistakes in each sentence. Find them and correct them.

1 Tom's bicycle is ~~newest~~ *newer* than ~~the bicycle of Bob~~ *Bob's bicycle*.

2 Monday is the worse day of the week for mine.

3 Mike and I live near Queen School, but my house is more far away from the school than him.

4 Brenda and Melissa aren't happy because their project isn't as easier as our.

5 Fred and Gail's computer is less expensively than the computer of Paul.

6 Mary's house has got most rooms than mine, and she cleans they every day!

g Communication

Work in pairs. How much do you know? Look at the prompts below, form sentences using the comparative and superlative forms and discuss with your partner, as in the examples. Then, check your answers.

vocabulary box

waterfall	polluted
continent	crowded

Victoria Falls **Niagara Falls** **Angel Falls**	**high / waterfall / world**
Europe **Asia** **Africa**	**big / continent / world**
Los Angeles **London** **Rio de Janeiro**	**polluted / city / three**

e.g. **A :** *I think Victoria Falls is the highest waterfall in the world.*
B : *I agree. / I don't agree. I think...*

Lake Ontario	**deep**	**Lake Baikal**
Tokyo	**crowded**	**New York**
Japan	**many islands**	**Indonesia**

e.g. **A :** *I think Lake Baikal is deeper than Lake Ontario.*
B : *I agree. / I don't agree. I think...*

Answers
- Angel Falls is the highest waterfall in the world.
- Asia is the biggest continent in the world.
- Los Angeles is the most polluted city of the three.
- Lake Baikal is deeper than Lake Ontario.
- Tokyo is more crowded than New York.
- Indonesia has got more islands than Japan.

h writing

Write a few sentences comparing three members of your family. Write about their appearance and the things they do. Use the words in the boxes.

tall short thin fat
funny interesting young
old beautiful good

play cook
drive work

beautifully well
carefully badly

....

....

....

....

....

....

....

....

Revision Units 1-5

a **Complete the blanks with the Present Simple or the Present Progressive of the verbs in brackets.**

1 ___*Is Betty taking*___ (Betty / take) French lessons this year?
2 Frank ______________ (often / not travel) by train, but he ______________ (travel) to Rome by train next week.
3 ______________ (your grandparents / visit) you tomorrow evening?
4 ______________ (you / know) Mrs Wilson?
5 How much ______________ (the jacket / cost) ?
6 The children ______________ (not play) computer games now.
7 The boys ______________ (not play) tennis twice a week. They ______________ (play) three times a week.

b **Complete the blanks with the Present Simple or the Present Progressive of the verbs in brackets.**

Juanita (**1**) ___*lives*___ (live) in Madrid. She (**2**) ______________ (work) at a supermarket, but she (**3**) ______________ (not like) it very much. She (**4**) ______________ (want) to find a better job.

Every morning she (**5**) ______________ (go) to work at seven o'clock. She (**6**) ______________ (usually/finish) at three but she (**7**) ______________ (sometimes/work) until four or five o'clock.

It is Monday today and it's half past twelve. Juanita (**8**) ______________ (not work) at the moment. She (**9**) ______________ (have) her lunch break. She (**10**) ______________ (sit) at a café with her friend Martha. They (**11**) ______________ (drink) soft drinks and they (**12**) ______________ (eat) salad. Martha (**13**) ______________ (tell) Juanita about her weekend. Martha (**14**) ______________ (always/do) something exciting at the weekend.

c **Complete the dialogues. Use a, an, the or - .**

1 **Mother:** Where are you going (**1**) ___–___ John?
John: I'm taking (**2**) ________ dog for (**3**) ________ walk.
Mother: It's raining. Take (**4**) ________ umbrella with you.
John: No, Ben has got (**5**) ________ black umbrella and I'm not taking (**6**) ________ red umbrella!

2 **Andrew:** I play (**7**) ________ guitar and my favourite subject at (**8**) ________ school is (**9**) ________ music.
Sheila: Really? I play (**10**) ________ guitar too. I've got (**11**) ________ old guitar.

3 **Mr Brown:** Are (**12**) ________ Smiths in (**13**) ________ France ?

Mrs Brown: Yes, they're in (**14**) ________ Paris at the moment. (**15**) ________ Kate called me yesterday. They're staying at (**16**) ________ hotel in (**17**) ________ city centre. I think it's (**18**) ________ Hilton. It's near (**19**) ________ River Seine. Yesterday, they had (**20**) ________ lunch at (**21**) ________ small restaurant near (**22**) ________ hotel. They love (**23**) ________ French food.

Mr Brown: Are they going anywhere else this summer?

Mrs Brown: Yes. They're visiting (**24**) ________ Netherlands.

d Circle the correct words.

There are a lot of **persons** / (**people**) at the circus tonight. There are lots of **family** / **families** with young **children** / **child**. Look at their **face** / **faces**. They're watching the clowns and they're smiling **happy** / **happily**. One clown has got red **hair** / **hairs** and big **foot** / **feet**! He's riding a **bicycle** / **bicycles** and he's holding a **box** / **boxes** of **tomato** / **tomatoes**. He wants to feed his **monkey** / **monkeys** but they don't want to eat. Now the clown is giving them a **glass** / **glasses** of **milk** / **milks**. Oh, no! They're **angry** / **angrily** and they're throwing their **glass** / **glasses** at the clown. Look! The clown is running away **quick** / **quickly**.

e Choose *a*, *b* or *c*.

1 Do you want to come to ___*my*___ party?
a. me (**b.**) my **c.** mine

2 Ask Paul about that T-shirt. I think it's ________ .
a. he **b.** him **c.** his

3 The dogs were hungry, so I gave ________ some biscuits.
a. their **b.** theirs **c.** them

4 ________ hotel room was nice and clean.
a. Our **b.** Ours **c.** Us

5 Somebody please help ________ ! We can't swim!
a. them **b.** ours **c.** us

6 That's Steve's football. ________ is at home.
a. My **b.** Me **c.** Mine

7 Kathy doesn't know about the test tomorrow. We must tell ________ .
a. her **b.** hers **c.** him

8 How often do you clean ________ bedroom?
a. you **b.** your **c.** yours

9 Look at that painting. Do you like ________ ?
a. him **b.** it **c.** its

10 That's not the Jones' car. ________ is in the garage.
a. Theirs **b.** Their **c.**Them

f Complete the blanks with much, many, a lot of, a few, a little, how much, how many.

Sarah: Do we need (**1**) ___*many*___ things from the supermarket to make the fruit cake?
Jessica: Let's see. Well, we've got some sugar, but not very (**2**) ______________ .
Sarah: OK, let's buy (**3**) ______________ more sugar. One packet, OK? Have we got any oranges?
Jessica: Yes, we've got (**4**) ______________ oranges but there are only (**5**) ______________ apples. Get some apples.
Sarah: (**6**) ______________ apples do we need?
Jessica: We don't need (**7**) ______________ , only two.
Sarah: Have we got any milk?
Jessica: Well, there's only (**8**) ______________ in the fridge.
Sarah: (**9**) ______________ milk do we need?
Jessica: We need (**10**) ______________ milk. Buy two cartons.
Sarah: What about eggs?
Jessica: Oh, there are (**11**) ______________ eggs in the fridge. Don't get any eggs because we haven't got (**12**) ______________ money, remember?
Sarah: All right.

g There is one mistake in each of the sentences below. Find it and correct it.

1 Have we got ~~no~~ *any* tea?
2 There aren't no people at the cinema.
3 There is anybody at home.
4 Can I have any coffee?
5 I can't find George somewhere.
6 Do you know nothing about dolphins?
7 Everyone student has got a bag.
8 There is nothing water in the fridge.
9 Ann come here, something wants to talk to you.
10 OK class, is someone here? Great, let's go!

h Complete the sentences. Use the correct form of the adjectives/adverbs in brackets.

1 My computer is ___*newer*___ than Ben's, but Peter's computer is the ______________ of all. (new)
2 Diane drives ______________ than Alice, but Anna drives the ______________ of the three. (carefully)
3 Chris wakes up as ______________ as Jane, but Nicky wakes up ______________ than them. (early)
4 I think tennis is as ______________ as basketball, but football is the ______________ of the three. (boring)
5 Exercise A was ______________ than exercise B, but this exercise was the ______________ of all. (difficult)

i **Look at the information and write two sentences. Use the comparative form of the adjectives and not as/so ... as ... . Begin with the words given.**

dress: £ 50
skirt: £ 35

1 cheap

The skirt *is cheaper than the dress.*

The dress *isn't as/so cheap as the skirt.*

Jack's house: built in 1935
Donna's house: built in 2000

2 modern

Jack's house ______________________

Donna's house ______________________

bike: 20 km/h
car: 80 km/h

3 fast

The car ______________________

The bike ______________________

Ted: 15 years old
Julie: 13 years old

4 old

Julie ______________________

Ted ______________________

j **Look at the pictures and write sentences. Use the possessive case and the adjectives in the box.**

~~old~~	new	long	small	dirty	heavy

woman / car

1 *The woman's car is old.*

Mark, Kelly / snake

2 ______________________

children / bags

3 ______________________

Helen, Kate / shoes

4 ______________________

boys / T-shirts

5 ______________________

baby / clothes

6 ______________________

Unit 6

Past Simple
Past Progressive

She was wearing a long white dress.

Read the text.

CHAPTER 1

It **was** very dark that night and it **was raining** heavily. Jamie and I **were driving** along a country road. Suddenly, the car **made** a funny noise and **stopped**.

We **didn't have** any more petrol. While Jamie **was looking** for a torch, I **got** out of the car. There **weren't** any houses around - just trees.

"Let's get some help," I said.

*

We **were walking** down the road when suddenly we **saw** a woman. She **was wearing** a long white dress. I **got** nearer and **screamed**:

"A ghost! A ghost!"

The sentences below are wrong. Rewrite them and correct them.

1 Jamie and the writer were driving in the city.

____

2 The car stopped because it was raining heavily.

____

3 Jamie and the writer were sitting in the car when they saw the woman.

____

4 When Jamie and the writer saw the woman, Jamie screamed.

____

Grammar

a Past Simple

We use the **Past Simple**:

- for actions that took place at a definite time in the past.
  I did my homework last night.
- for past habits or for actions that took place repeatedly in the past.
  I often went to the cinema when I was young.

- We form the Past Simple of **regular verbs** by adding **-ed** to the base form of the verb in **all** persons.
- Each **irregular** verb forms the **affirmative** form of the **Past Simple** in a different way. You will find these verbs in the Table of Irregular Verbs on pages 152-153.
- All verbs (regular and Irregular) form the **interrogative** and **negative** form of the **Past Simple** with **did / didn't + base form**.

Affirmative	Negative	
	FULL FORMS	SHORT FORMS
I worked / ate	I did not work / eat	I didn't work / eat
He/She/It worked / ate	He/She/It did not work / eat	He/She/It didn't work / eat
We/You/They worked / ate	We/You/They did not work / eat	We/You/They didn't work / eat

Interrogative	Short Answers	
Did I work / eat?	Yes, I did.	No, I didn't.
Did he/she/it work / eat?	Yes, he/she/it did.	No, he/she/it didn't.
Did we/you/they work / eat?	Yes, we/you/they did.	No, we/you/they didn't.

Spelling

dance → danced				
stop → stopped		shout → shouted		
prefer → preferred	**but**	visit → visited		
study → studied		play → played		
travel → travelled		sail → sailed		

Time Expressions

yesterday, the day before yesterday
last night/week/month/year, etc.
two days/hours/years, etc. ago
on Monday / in March / in 1998, etc.
last Sunday, last March, etc.

b Past Progressive

We use the **Past Progressive**:

- for an action that was happening in the past and was interrupted by another action. The **longer action** is in the **Past Progressive** and the **shorter action** (which interrupted the longer one) is in the **Past Simple**. We usually use **while** and **when**.
  I was having a bath when the phone rang.
- for actions that were taking place at the same time in the past.
  She was reading a book while he was listening to music.
- to describe background scenes to a story.
  It was snowing and Sue was trying to start the car. Suddenly, she saw...
- for actions that were taking place at a specific point of time in the past.
  I was watching a film at ten o'clock last night.

Affirmative	Negative	
	FULL FORMS	SHORT FORMS
I was eating	I was not eating	I wasn't eating
You were eating	You were not eating	You weren't eating
He was eating	He was not eating	He wasn't eating
She was eating	She was not eating	She wasn't eating
It was eating	It was not eating	It wasn't eating
We were eating	We were not eating	We weren't eating
You were eating	You were not eating	You weren't eating
They were eating	They were not eating	They weren't eating

Interrogative	Short Answers	
Was I eating?	Yes, I was.	No, I wasn't.
Were you eating?	Yes, you were.	No, you weren't.
Was he eating?	Yes, he was.	No, he wasn't.
Was she eating?	Yes, she was.	No, she wasn't.
Was it eating?	Yes, it was.	No, it wasn't.
Were we eating?	Yes, we were.	No, we weren't.
Were you eating?	Yes, you were.	No, you weren't.
Were they eating?	Yes, they were.	No, they weren't.

Notes:

- To describe past habits or actions that happened repeatedly in the past we use the Past Simple, **not** the Past Progressive.
  I played football every day when I was young.
- **Stative verbs** are not usually used in the Past Progressive.

activities

a **Look at the pictures and the prompts. Write questions and answers. Use the Past Simple.**

1 Karen / stay / hotel / last summer / ?

Did Karen stay at a hotel
last summer?
Yes, she did.
____

2 Mary and Tom / wash / bikes / yesterday / ?

____
____
____
____

3 Tina / send / Jane / letter / two weeks ago / ?

____
____
____
____

4 Dennis / go / bank / yesterday morning / ?

____
____
____
____

5 Lucy and Sue / have / lunch / restaurant / yesterday / ?

____
____
____
____

6 girls / meet / library / noon / ?

____
____
____
____

b What was everybody doing when Mrs Hunt came home from work yesterday afternoon? Look at the picture and complete the sentences with the Past Progressive of the verbs in the box.

read
run
~~cook~~
sleep
sit
play
cry

1 Mr Hunt *was cooking* dinner.

2 John ______________ computer games.

3 Sheila ______________ the newspaper.

4 The baby ______________ .

5 Grandfather and grandmother ______________ in the garden.

6 The dog ______________ .

7 The cats ______________ around the living room.

c Look at the pictures and the prompts. Write questions and answers. Use the Past Progressive.

1 Rob / play / football / 6:00 / yesterday / ?

Was Rob playing football at 6:00 yesterday?
No, he wasn't. He was playing basketball.

2 children / sleep / 10:00 / last night / ?

____
____
____
____

3 it / rain / last Thursday / ?

____
____
____
____

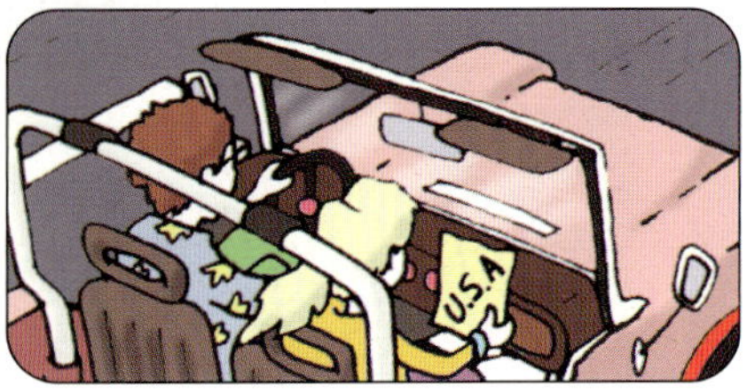

4 the Wilsons / travel / around / Europe / two months ago / ?

___

___

___

___

5 Diane / wear / dress / school / yesterday / ?

___

___

___

___

6 Chris / do / homework / yesterday afternoon / ?

___

___

___

___

d Complete the sentences with the Past Simple or the Past Progressive of the verbs in brackets.

1 We *were eating* (eat) lunch when the doorbell *rang* (ring).

2 ___ (you/walk) to school when it ___ (start) raining?

3 I ___ (not buy) the car last year, I ___ (buy) it last month.

4 While I ___ (study) for a test yesterday, my brother ___ (have) fun with his friends.

5 While my father ___ (drive) to work this morning, he ___ (see) an elephant in the middle of the road!

6 When Mr Trent ___ (meet) his wife, he ___ (work) as an English teacher in Paris.

7 Kelly ___ (park) her car, ___ (get) out and ___ (walk) into the bookshop.

8 What ___ (John/do) while you ___ (skate)?

9 My friends and I ___ (play) a board game when the lights ___ (go) out.

10 What ___ (you/say)? I ___ (not listen) to you.

e Look at the pictures and write sentences. Use the verbs below the pictures in the Past Simple or the Past Progressive and when.

1 clean / see

She was cleaning the garage

when she saw a spider.

___

2 swim / ring

___

___

___

3 fish / see

___

___

___

4 ride / start raining

5 walk / find

6 watch / hear

f can you remember?

Circle the correct words.

Yesterday Kevin (**1**) **lazy** / **lazily** got out of bed and looked at his watch.

"Oh, no! I'm late for school again! I must try to wake up (**2**) **earlier** / **earliest**," he thought.

He ate his breakfast (**3**) **quicker** / **quickly** and left. He (**4**) **running** / **was running** to the bus stop when he saw something on the road. It was a gold watch. He put it in his pocket and (**5**) **went** / **was going** to the police station.

Kevin (**6**) **was telling** / **told** a police officer about the watch when he heard a voice behind him.

"That's my watch!" said a man. He took the watch and asked: "Where (**7**) **were you find** / **did you find** it?"

"On the road," said Kevin.

"Thank you, young man. You did (**8**) **good** / **well**. I'm the (**9**) **luckier** / **luckiest** man in town because this watch is very expensive," he said and (**10**) **gave** / **was giving** Kevin £100. "Come on, I'll drive you to school and explain everything to your teacher."

Kevin smiled (**11**) **happy** / **happily** and walked out of the police station.

g Communication

Work in pairs.
- **Choose six of the activities in the vocabulary box to complete the diary on the next page for last weekend, but don't tell your partner.**
- **Ask your partner questions, as in the example, to find out what he/she did last weekend and when he/she was doing these activities. Write his/her answers on the diary.**
- **Then, answer your partner's questions and compare your answers.**

vocabulary box

play table tennis
make cake
plant flowers
send e-mails
prepare dinner
paint bedroom
build dog-house
fix bike
clean garage

e.g. **A :** *What did you do last Saturday?*
B : *I..., ... and ...*
A : *Were you ... at eleven o' clock in the morning?*
B : *Yes, I was. / No, I wasn't. I was...*

My diary

Saturday:	11 am
	3 pm
	8 pm
Sunday:	11 am
	3 pm
	8 pm

_______________'s diary

Saturday:	11 am
	3 pm
	8 pm
Sunday:	11 am
	3 pm
	8 pm

h writing

Look at the comic strip and the prompts below and write what happened.

- man / walk / with / dog / near lake
- man / listen / music

- suddenly / monster / come out / lake
- man / not see or hear / monster

- dog / see / monster
- dog / bark at / monster
- monster / be / scared / and / jump / lake / again

One day, a man...
....
....
....
....
....
....
....

Unit 7

Prepositions of Time
Prepositions of Place
Prepositions of Movement

A camping holiday

Read Sandy's letter to her friend Kelly.

Dear Kelly,

How are you? I'm on a camping holiday **at** the moment and it's wonderful. The campsite is **next to** a river, **near** a forest. We sleep **in** small cabins and we have all our meals **in** the dining hall. The dining hall is **in** the main building **opposite** our cabins.

We do lots of exciting things every day. You won't believe what we did **on** Sunday. **After** breakfast we walked for three kilometres **along** the river and we came **to** a high bridge. Then we jumped **off** the bridge **into** the water. I was scared, but it was very exciting. I want to do it again!

Bye for now,
Sandy

Now write the prepositions under the correct heading.

Time	Place	Movement
______	______	______
______	______	______
______	______	______
	______	______

Grammar

a Prepositions of Time

- **at:** to show the **exact time**: *at seven o'clock*
  in the expressions: *at noon, at night, at midnight, at the weekend(s), at Christmas, at Easter, at the moment*
- **on:** with the **days of the week**: *on Monday / on Mondays*
  with **dates**: *on 26 February*
  in the expressions: *on Christmas Day/Eve, on New Year's Day/Eve, on my birthday, on a hot day, on Saturday evening, etc.*
- **in:** with **months** and **seasons**: *in June / in (the) spring*
  with **years** and **centuries**: *in 1995 / in the 21st century*
  with **periods of the day**: *in the morning / in the afternoon / in the evening*
  but *on Monday morning/afternoon/evening*
- **during** *I met him during the summer.*
- **before** *He arrived before midnight.*
- **after** *She left after lunch.*

b Prepositions of Place

on
*The book is **on** the table.*

in
*The pen is **in** the box.*

at
*A man is **at** the door.*

over
*There's a bridge **over** the river.*

under
The *dog is sleeping **under** the table.*

in front of
*There's a garden **in front of** the house.*

behind
*Don't stand **behind** me.*

near
*My house is **near** the school.*

next to / beside
*Laura sits **next to / beside** me at school.*

opposite
*My house is **opposite** the park.*

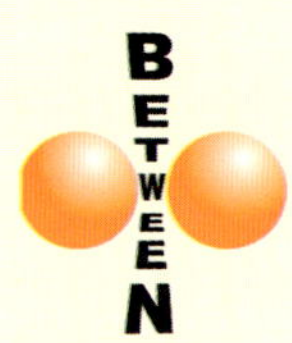

between
*The post office is **between** the library and the school.*

among
*The teacher was standing **among** the students.*

Notes:

- **In** is used before names of **cities**, **countries**, **continents**.
  She lives in Paris / in France. Spain is in Europe.
- **At** is used for **small places** and for **addresses**, when the number is mentioned. It is also used in expressions **at school**, **at home**, **at work**, **at the door**, **at the bus stop**, **at the table**, **at my desk**, etc.
  Wendy is at the cinema. Jane lives at 4 Rose Street.
- **On** is used in the expressions: **on the left**, **on the right**.

C Prepositions of Movement

into
A bird flew ***into*** *the room.*

out of
She walked ***out of*** *the room.*

from **to**
Tomorrow we're driving ***from*** *London* ***to*** *Brighton.*

over
The cat is jumping ***over*** *the fence.*

up
She ran ***up*** *the stairs.*

down
She ran ***down*** *the stairs.*

across
Walk ***across*** *the street.*

along
We walked ***along*** *the river.*

through
The train went ***through*** *the tunnel.*

off
Penny jumped ***off*** *the bridge.*

round
The horse ran ***round*** *the lake.*

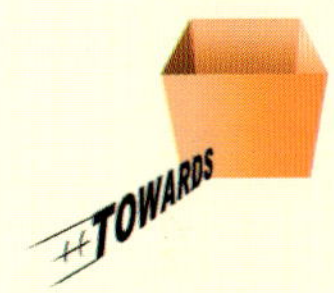

towards
The children came ***towards*** *me.*

activities

a Complete the blanks with prepositions of time.

New Message

File Edit View Insert Format Tools Message Help

From:

To: Polly

Subject: New Year Cruise!!!

Dear Polly,

Do you want to do something special (**1**) ___*on*___ New Year's Eve? Then join us on a Star Cruise along the Thames. The cruise begins (**2**) _________ 6:30 pm (**3**) _________ Sunday, December 31st. There will be a special dinner (**4**) _________ the evening, and then the party starts. There will be a fireworks display (**5**) _________ midnight, and the party will continue all night long. (**6**) _________ New Year's Day there will be a special 'Celebration' Breakfast. (**7**) _______ breakfast you can enjoy lots of different games. There will be lots of music, food and drink (**8**) _________ the day, too. What do you think?

New Message

File Edit View Insert Format Tools Message Help

From:

To: Jeff

Subject: Summer holiday

Dear Jeff,

I can't come to Malta with you on holiday (**9**) ________ August because I'm going to be very busy all summer. However, I go to different places (**10**) ________ weekends. I usually leave (**11**) ________ Friday evening and come back late (**12**) ________ night (**13**) ________ Sunday. I don't like coming back (**14**) ________ Monday morning because I hate waking up early (**15**) _____ the morning. Anyway, (**16**) ________ the 20th of July I'm going to Bath. Would you like to come?

b Complete the blanks with the prepositions of movement in the box.

across ~~to~~ to through into into round up off along out of over

1 Wendy goes ___*to*___ school by bus.

2 Our cat jumped ______________ the fence ______________ the neighbour's garden.

3 Paul fell ______________ his bicycle and hurt his knee.

4 Kerry came ______________ the supermarket with six heavy bags.

5 Who swam the fastest ______________ the lake?

6 It's very easy to get ______________ the Pine Hotel. Drive ______________ Station Road and turn left ______________ Forest Road. After about 200 metres you'll see Rosewood forest. The road goes ______________ the forest, ______________ a small lake and ______________ a hill. The Pine Hotel is at the end of the road, near the top of the hill.

c Look at the pictures and complete the blanks with prepositions of place.

1 A boy is standing ___*on*___ a bridge. There is a boat __________ the bridge. There are some people __________ the boat.

2 Carla is standing __________ her friends. She is the girl __________ the boy in the red jacket and the boy with the glasses. A tall girl is standing __________ Carla.

3 __________ my bedroom, my bed is __________ the window. The window is __________ the door. My favourite poster is __________ the wall __________ my bed.

4 My car is ________ the car park. It's ________ the blue car and ________ the white van.

5 The post office is ________ the library and ________ the bank.

6 Kathy isn't ________ work. She is ________ home and she's having breakfast ________ the kitchen.

d Choose *a*, *b* or *c*.

1 Are you having a party ___*on*___ your birthday?
a. in **(b.)** on **c.** at

2 The children rode their bicycles ________ the hill.
a. down **b.** from **c.** out of

3 There were two World Wars ________ the 20th century.
a. on **b.** at **c.** in

4 The runners jumped ________ the wall.
a. over **b.** across **c.** opposite

5 We bought this car ________ 1999.
a. on **b.** at **c.** in

6 George lives ________ 25 Main Street.
a. at **b.** in **c.** on

7 We are meeting Tina ________ the airport.
a. into **b.** at **c.** on

8 I saw Ben five minutes ago. He was walking ________ the swimming pool.
a. from **b.** towards **c.** off

9 My brother is studying ________ England.
a. in **b.** at **c.** to

10 Andorra is a small country ________ Europe.
a. towards **b.** in **c.** at

e can you remember?

Expand the notes below and write sentences. Use the Past Simple, the Past Progressive and the prepositions in the box.

on	beside	~~off~~	during	along	to	at

1 Penny / clean / room / vase / fall / table
Penny was cleaning the room when the vase fell off the table.

2 my friends / walk / street / when / they / see / accident
____

3 Leo / sit / Sheila / when / I / arrive / cinema
____

4 Harry and I / talk / lesson / when / teacher / see / us

____

5 I / travel / London / when / I / lose / wallet

____

6 Susan / cook / when / Jill / call / her / Monday evening

____

f Communication

Work in pairs. Imagine that your house is one of the five houses on the map below. Give your partner directions to your house. Use words / phrases from the vocabulary box.

vocabulary box

turn left / right
turn into ... Street
go straight

town hall
shopping centre
railway station

e.g. *Walk straight along Elm Road and turn left/right into... Then...*
My house is opposite/ next to / between...

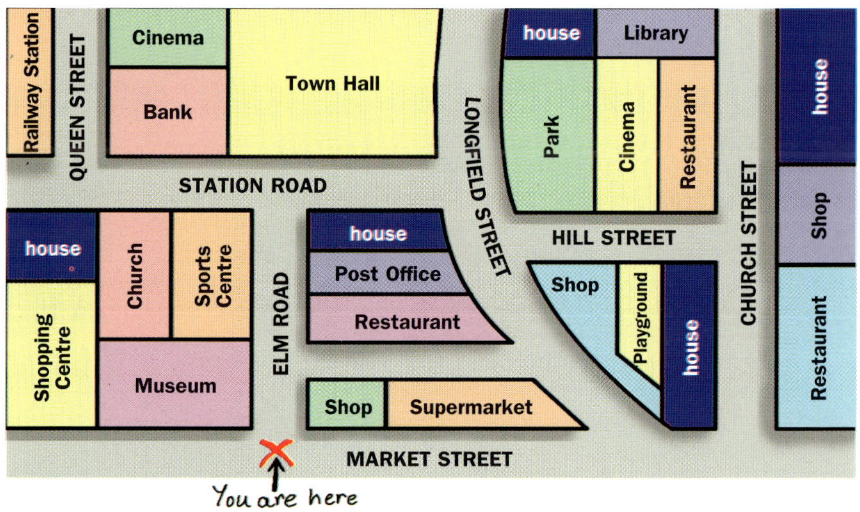

g writing

How do you get from your house to your school? Write at least three sentences.

Walk along ....

....

....

....

....

....

....

....

Unit 8

Relative Clauses
Relative Pronouns (who, which, that, whose)

A holiday picture

Jenny is showing Michael a picture from last year's summer holidays. Look at the picture and complete the dialogue with the phrases a - d.

a. which you gave me for my birthday

b. who's wearing the big green hat

c. whose dog looks like a sausage

d. that I met on the beach

Michael: Where's your sister? I can't see her.
Jenny: She's the girl ____________________ .
Michael: She looks very funny. Who's that next to you?
Jenny: That's Chris, the boy ____________________ .
Michael: Yes, you told me about him. Is that your T-shirt he's wearing?
Jenny: Yes, it's the T-shirt ____________________ .
Michael: That's right. Why is he wearing it?
Jenny: Well, do you see that fat man?
Michael: There are two fat men.
Jenny: The man ____________________ .
Michael: Yes, what about him?
Jenny: Well, he was sitting near us and his dog jumped on Chris and ruined his clothes. So I gave him my T-shirt.

Grammar

a Relative Clauses

- **Relative Clauses** give information about the subject or object of the main clause. They are introduced by the relative pronouns **who**, **which**, **that** and **whose**.

b Relative Pronouns

- **Who** is used for people.

  That's the girl. She gave me this pen. → *That's the girl **who** gave me this pen.*
  That's the boy. I met him at your party. → *That's the boy **who** I met at your party.*

- **Which** is used for animals, things and abstract nouns.

  That's the dog. It barks every night. → *That's the dog **which** barks every night.*
  The car is blue. We bought it last week. → *The car **which** we bought last week is blue.*

- **That** is used for people, animals, things and abstract nouns. It can replace **who** and **which**.

  *That's the girl **who** gave me this pen.* → *That's the girl **that** gave me this pen.*
  *The car **which** we bought last week is blue.* → *The car **that** we bought last week is blue.*

- **Whose** shows possession and replaces **possessive adjectives**. It is used mainly for people and animals.

  That's the boy. His father is a doctor. → *That's the boy **whose** father is a doctor.*

Notes:

- The relative pronouns **who**, **which** and **that** can be omitted when they refer to the **object** of the main clause.

  That's the woman. I met her last week. → *That's the woman **who/that** I met last week.*
  That's the woman I met last week.

  Come and see the house. We bought it last year. → *Come and see the house **which/that** we bought last year.*
  Come and see the house we bought last year.

- That's the dog which ~~it~~ barks every night.
  That's the woman who I met ~~her~~ last week.

activities

a Complete the sentences with who or which.

1 Mrs Miles is a teacher ___*who*___ teaches geography.
2 Mary, show me the dress ______________ you bought yesterday.
3 A baker is someone ______________ makes and sells bread.
4 The girl ______________ works at the Internet Café is my cousin.
5 A koala is an animal ______________ eats eucalyptus leaves.
6 Ricky Martin is the singer ______________ we saw at the concert.
7 Spanish is a language ______________ many people like.
8 The cake ______________ my mum made yesterday was delicious.

b **Match the two halves of the sentences. Then join them using who, which or that to make sentences. If the pronouns can be omitted, put them in brackets.**

1 A photographer is a person...
2 The 'Chunnel' is the tunnel...
3 Cricket is a sport...
4 Leonardo Da Vinci was the artist...
5 The kangaroo is an animal...
6 A watch is something...
7 Pilots are people...
8 A doctor is someone...

a ... many people in England play.
b ... tells people the time.
c ... takes pictures.
d ... lives in Australia.
e ... people see when they are ill.
f ... connects France with England.
g ... painted the Mona Lisa.
h ... fly planes.

1 *A photographer is a person who/that takes pictures.*
2 ______________________
3 ______________________
4 ______________________
5 ______________________
6 ______________________
7 ______________________
8 ______________________

c **There is an extra word in each of the sentences below. Cross it out.**

1 That's the girl who ~~she~~ lives next door.
2 The book that I bought it is very interesting.
3 This is my uncle whose daughter she won the photography competition last year.
4 Those are my neighbours whose their dog barks all night.
5 The man who he discovered Australia was James Cook.
6 The penguin is a bird which it lives at the South Pole.

d **Look at the pictures and the speech bubbles and write sentences as in the example. Use whose.**

1 *That's the man whose parrot ate my flowers.*

2 ______________________

3 ______________________

4

____

____

5

____

____

6

____

____

e **Join the sentences. Use who, which, that or whose. If the pronouns can be omitted, put them in brackets.**

1 Do you like the poster? I made it for my school project.

Do you like the poster (which/that) I made for my school project?

2 Last week Sue met a boy. He's from the Netherlands.

____

3 Look at this ring. I found it in the garden.

____

4 My best friend has got a sister. Her hair is pink.

____

5 My parents live in a town. It's near a beautiful beach.

____

6 Brian went to the cinema with a girl. He likes her a lot.

____

f ## can you remember?

Complete the blanks using who, which, whose and the prepositions in the box.

in at ~~on~~ during with in in to

Lisa: What did you do (**1**) ___*on*___ Saturday, Anna?

Anna: Not much. (**2**) ____________ the evening I watched a film (**3**) ____________ I really liked. It was about a boy (**4**) ____________ family went (**5**) ____________ France but they forgot to take him (**6**) ____________ them. The film shows what happened (**7**) ____________ the three days that he was alone. What did you do?

Lisa: I stayed (**8**) _______________ home and watched TV, too. I watched a very interesting documentary about India. You see, India is a country (**9**) _______________ I want to visit (**10**) _______________ the future.

Anna: I'm reading a book (**11**) _______________ you would like, then. The woman (**12**) _______________ wrote it lived (**13**) _______________ India for many years. You can borrow it after I finish it, OK?

g Communication

Work in pairs.

Student A Go to page 138

Student B Go to page 146

vocabulary box

take pictures
exercise
get on
get off
chase
cross

h writing

Make up a quiz. Complete the sentences below as in the examples. Then, give your quiz to someone and check his/her answers.

KNOWLEDGE QUIZ

1	He was the man who discovered America.	
2	It's a machine people use to wash clothes.	
3	It's an animal...	
4	He's the person...	
5	It's a thing...	
6	It's a bird...	
7	...	
8	...	

Unit 9

Reflexive/Emphatic Pronouns
Which?
One/Ones

How much do you care?

Do you care about yourself more than you care about others? Do this quiz and find out.

1 Yesterday you bought a camera for your brother, but it doesn't work. What do you do?

A. You return it to the shop and ask for a new **one**.
B. You give it to your brother. He **himself** can return it to the shop.

2 Your brother asks for help with his homework. Which of the following do you say?

A. "I'll help you, but next time you must do it **by yourself**."
B. "I don't have any time."

3 A classmate invites you to a party, but he doesn't invite your best friend. What do you do?

A. You don't go to the party. You go out with your best friend.
B. You go to the party **by yourself**. Your best friend can do something else to enjoy **herself**.

4 Somebody brought you a puppy for your birthday last week. Now it's really dirty. What do you do?

A. You give it a bath.
B. You don't do anything. Dogs can clean **themselves**.

Now check your answers.

More As : You are a good friend and care about others.
More Bs : Don't think only about yourself! Do things for others, too.

Grammar

a Reflexive Pronouns / Emphatic Pronouns

Reflexive pronouns show that an action returns to the person who does it. In other words, the object of the verb is the same as its subject.

Bob cut himself with the bread knife.

Personal Pronouns		Reflexive Pronouns
SUBJECT	OBJECT	
I	me	myself
you	you	yourself
he	him	himself
she	her	herself
it	it	itself
we	us	ourselves
you	you	yourselves
they	them	themselves

Reflexive Pronouns are used:

- after transitive verbs (= verbs that take an object).
  Mary fell down and hurt herself.
- after prepositions.
  George is talking to himself.

Note: ● **by + reflexive pronoun** shows that someone is alone or does something without help.
What are you doing here all by yourself? *My daughter walks by herself now.*

- Sometimes **reflexive pronouns** are used to give emphasis to the subject or the object of the verb. Then they are called **Emphatic Pronouns**.
- **Emphatic Pronouns** are placed immediately after the word we want to emphasise, or at the end of the sentence.
  I myself painted this picture. (The emphasis is on the subject.)
  I painted this picture myself. (The emphasis is on the subject.)
  I want to see the teacher herself. (The emphasis is on the object.)

b Which?

We use questions beginning with **which** when we want to identify a person or thing from a limited number of people or similar things.

Which book do you want to borrow, Hard Times *or* Oliver Twist*?*
Which of these three girls is your sister?

c One/Ones

- The pronoun **one/ones** is used when we don't want to repeat a noun that has already been mentioned.
  I bought the black dress, not the blue one.
- **One** replaces a singular countable noun. **Ones** replaces a plural countable noun. **One/ones** do not replace uncountable nouns.
  Those aren't my shoes. The ones under the table are mine.
- We can use the pronoun **one/ones** to answer questions that begin with **which**.
  Which bicycle is yours? *The green one.*

activities

a Complete the blanks with reflexive pronouns.

1 Ted is crying because he fell down and cut ___*himself*___ on a piece of glass.

2 **Bob:** Did you enjoy ________________ at the party last night?

Liz: Oh, yes! I had a great time.

3 Children, be careful or you will hurt ________________ !

4 **John:** It's raining! We can't go out tonight.

Mary: Let's make ________________ some tea and sit by the fire.

5 **Emma:** What happened to you?

George: I burnt ________________ while I was cooking last night.

6 There's something wrong with Kate. She's talking to ________________ !

7 Fiona and Julie buy ________________ new clothes every month.

8 My brother calls ________________ Tommy, but mum calls him Thomas.

b Complete the sentences with reflexive pronouns if they are necessary.

1 We really enjoyed ___*ourselves*___ at the party.

2 Jack invited ________________ my sister to his party.

3 I was climbing the tree when I fell and hurt ________________ .

4 The car crashed ________________ into a tree.

5 Vicky bought ________________ me a great book for my birthday last year.

6 Jason doesn't like to talk about ________________ . He's shy.

7 Connie cut ________________ a few pieces of cake for the children.

c Look at the pictures and the prompts and write questions and answers.

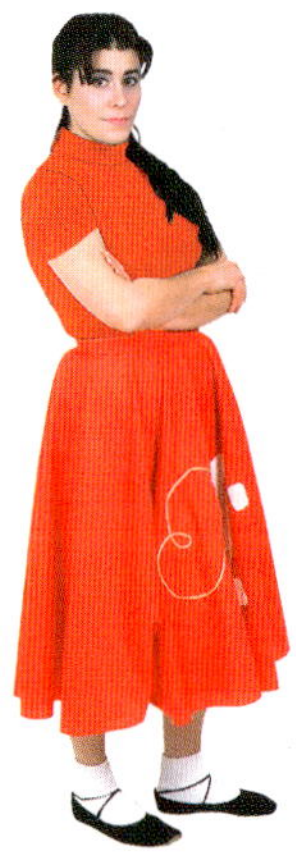

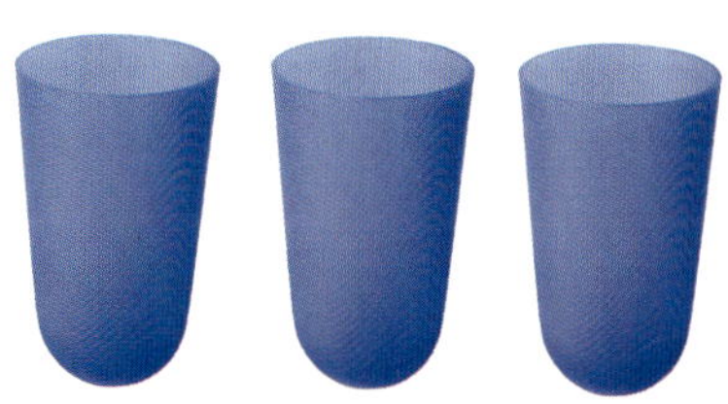

1 bag / be / yours / ?

Which bag is yours?

The brown one.

2 dress / Mary / wear / now / ?

____

____

3 glasses / David / break / yesterday / ?

____

____

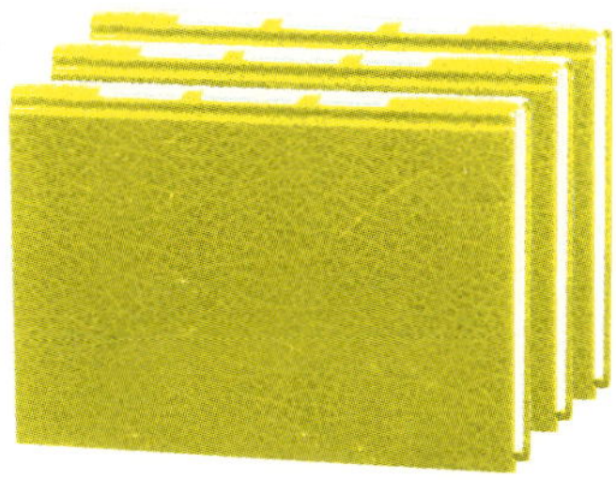

4 books / be / the teacher's / ?

____

____

5 watches / girls / like / ?

____

____

6 umbrella / May / carry / now / ?

____

____

d Circle the correct words.

1 Mary is at the library. I saw **her** / **herself** there two hours ago.
2 This cake is delicious! Did you make it **you** / **yourself**?
3 Beth, what happened to **you** / **yourself**? Please tell **me** / **myself**!
4 Danny, don't help your sister with her homework. She can do it **her** / **herself**.
5 Don't worry! I'll talk to David **me** / **myself**.
6 Donna is spending the summer in Spain! Can you believe **it** / **itself**?
7 Some people like to stay at home by **them** / **themselves**.
8 My dog Skip gets scared easily. We never leave **him** / **himself** at home by **him** / **himself**.
9 Laura's parents live very far away. She only visits **them** / **themselves** once a year.
10 Jim and I are going to the cinema tonight. Can you drive **us** / **ourselves** there, dad?

e can you remember?

Complete the sentences. Use relative pronouns (who, which, that) and reflexive / emphatic pronouns (myself, yourself etc.)

1 Vincent Van Gogh is a famous artist *who / that* painted a picture of *himself* .
2 Is that the dress ______________ you made by ______________ ?
3 A cat is an animal ______________ usually cleans ______________ .
4 My brother and I are among the people ______________ never buy any vegetables. We grow all our vegetables ______________ .
5 Mrs Brown is the old lady ______________ lives by ______________ in a huge house.
6 John and Tom are the boys ______________ stayed in a tent in a forest for a week. During that week they did everything by ______________ .

f Communication

Work in groups.
- Take turns to ask the others in the group questions, using the ideas in the chart below and *reflexive pronouns*, as in the example.
- Note your answers on the chart and answer the questions for yourself.
- Report the results of the survey to your class.

vocabulary box

repair
iron
grow
cut

SURVEY				
	Name:	Name:	Name:	Name:
you / clean / bedroom				
you / wash / clothes				
father / repair / car				
mother / iron / clothes				
parents / grow / vegetables				
you / cut / hair				

e.g. **A :** *Do you clean your bedroom (by) yourself?*
B : *Yes, I do. / No, I don't. My mother cleans it.*

Results: *Jane and Jack clean their bedrooms by themselves but Tom doesn't clean his himself. His mother helps him.*

g writing

What things do you do by yourself? What things do the members of your family do by themselves? Write 4-5 sentences using reflexive pronouns.

....

....

....

....

....

....

....

....

....

Revision Units 6-9

a **Look at the picture below. What were the students doing when the teacher walked into the classroom? Complete the sentences with the Past Progressive of the verbs in the box.**

talk   draw   read   make   ~~do~~   look

1 Kevin *was doing* his homework.
2 Lyn ____________________ to Betty.
3 George and Tom ____________________ paper planes.
4 Susan ____________________ out of the window.
5 Mary and Philip ____________________ magazines.
6 Rob ____________________ a picture.

b **Complete the sentences below with the Past Simple or the Past Progressive of the verbs in brackets.**

1 Donna *was washing* (wash) the dishes at seven o'clock last night.
2 Ann and Kitty ____________________ (not watch) TV when Roger ____________________ (come). They ____________________ (study).
3 While Beth and Diane ____________________ (listen) to music, the phone ____________________ (ring).
4 Tina ____________________ (prepare) dinner while Ron and Luke ____________________ (clean) the house.
5 **Keith:** What ____________________ (James / do) when he ____________________ (break) the vase?
Michael: He ____________________ (buy) a new one.
6 We often ____________________ (play) computer games together when we ____________________ (be) young.
7 **Melissa:** ____________________ (it / rain) when you ____________________ (arrive) in Finland?
Christine: No, it ____________________ (snow).
8 Janet ____________________ (get off) the bus and ____________________ (walk) towards her house.

c Complete the blanks with the Past Simple or the Past Progressive of the verbs in brackets.

Last year my friend Don and I (**1**) ___*decided*___ (decide) to go to Nepal on holiday. We (**2**) ____________ (want) to go climbing in the Himalayas. One night, we (**3**) ____________ (try) to find a place to camp when we (**4**) ____________ (see) some strange footprints. We (**5**) ____________ (think) they (**6**) ____________ (be) a bear's footprints. Anyway, a little later we (**7**) ____________ (find) a place to camp near a lake. While I (**8**) ____________ (get) water from the lake, Don (**9**) ____________ (cook). Suddenly, he (**10**) ____________ (scream)! I (**11**) ____________ (turn) around but he (**12**) ____________ (not be) there anymore! I (**13**) ____________ (call) out his name, but there (**14**) ____________ (be) no answer. I (**15**) ____________ (run) towards our tent when I (**16**) ____________ (see) a strange creature. It (**17**) ____________ (be) huge and it (**18**) ____________ (carry) Don! They (**19**) ____________ (disappear) into the trees and I never (**20**) ____________ (see) Don again.

d Look at the picture, read the text below and complete the blanks. Choose *a*, *b* or *c*.

(**1**) ___*At*___ 8 o'clock (**2**) ____________ Monday morning I was standing (**3**) ____________ the bus stop which is (**4**) ____________ Rose Café and I saw an accident. This is what happened.

A bus was going (**5**) ____________ Arbour Street. A blue car was coming (**6**) ____________ Birch Street. There was a boy (**7**) ____________ a bicycle (**8**) ____________ the blue car. I think he was going (**9**) ____________ school because he had a bag. At the same time, a man was walking (**10**) ____________ Arbour Street. He didn't see the bus. When the bus driver saw the man, he stopped. However, the blue car crashed into the bus and the boy fell (**11**) ____________ his bicycle.

1	(**a.**) At	**b.** On	**c.** In	**7**	**a.** over	**b.** on	**c.** at
2	**a.** in	**b.** at	**c.** on	**8**	**a.** opposite	**b.** beside	**c.** behind
3	**a.** in	**b.** to	**c.** at	**9**	**a.** to	**b.** in	**c.** at
4	**a.** next	**b.** near	**c.** along	**10**	**a.** along	**b.** across	**c.** among
5	**a.** along	**b.** through	**c.** over	**11**	**a.** from	**b.** down	**c.** off
6	**a.** round	**b.** from	**c.** off				

e Complete the sentences with who, whose or which.

There are lots of interesting people in my neighbourhood. Let me tell you about some of them. First, there's May. She's the girl ___*who*___ won the lottery last week. Then there is Mrs Green. She lives in a house with a big garden ____________ has got twenty trees. Hans is a boy ____________ father is a famous scientist and Kelly and Jenny are two girls ____________ mother is a pilot. There is also Mr Benson, a man ____________ can speak nine languages. Finally, there's Miss Danson. She has got a monkey ____________ plays the piano!

f **Join the sentences below. Use who, which, that or whose. If the pronouns can be omitted, put them in brackets.**

1 There's my cousin. She loves cherries.
There's my cousin who loves cherries.

2 I paint pictures. My friends like them.
____

3 This is my neighbour. Her brother plays the drums.
____

4 I visited a museum. It's very big.
____

5 These are the students. I taught them last year.
____

g **Complete the blanks with reflexive, emphatic or object pronouns.**

1 Mary looked at *herself* in the mirror before she left the house.
2 How did you hurt ________ ? Did you have an accident?
3 My father fixed our car ________. Nobody helped ________.
4 My aunt never leaves her children at home by ________.
5 Penny and I took the pictures ________. Do you like ________?
6 Stephanie, I can't find the answer by ________. Please help ________.
7 My sister and I met the famous actress Alice Lee ________ and we talked to ________!
8 The film ________ isn't very good but the music is excellent. I really liked ________!
9 Linda isn't at home. We saw ________ at the shops but she didn't see ________.
10 The girls chose the colour for their bedroom ________ . Do you like ________?

h **Look at the prompts below. Form questions with which and answers with one or ones.**

1 dog / be / yours? — brown ✓ black ☐
Which dog is yours? The brown one.

2 chairs / you / buy / yesterday? — green ☐ yellow ✓
____

3 trainers / you / like? — cheap ☐ expensive ✓
____

4 car / be / Helen's? — small ✓ big ☐
____

Unit 10

Present Perfect Simple

Have you improved your English?

Read the text below.

What's the best way to improve your English?

Here's what some students of English have done to improve their English.

Kanit from Thailand
I think it's very important to visit English speaking countries. **I've already been** to Australia on holiday and this **has helped** me improve my English a lot. I **haven't visited** the UK yet, but I hope I'll go there next year.

Kostas from Greece
I've never been abroad, but lots of foreign tourists visit Greece every year, so I can speak English with them. **I've met** lots of interesting people from England and the USA. A boy from New York **has invited** me there. I'm going next month!

Irina from Poland
I **have had** a penfriend from England for nine months now and I think it's good practice to read and write letters in English. Reading English books is also useful and it's fun, too. **I've just finished** a great book! It's called *Great Expectations*.

What have you done to improve your English? Write sentences using the notes below and some of the words in the box.

already	yet	never	just	for

1 travel / England

____

2 read / English book

____

3 have / English-speaking penfriend

____

Grammar

Present Perfect Simple

We use the **Present Perfect Simple**:

- for actions which happened in the past, but we don't mention when exactly. The results of these actions are obvious in the present.
  I have visited Rome before and I can tell you a lot about it.
  You can't have a cake because Ted has eaten all of them.

Time Expressions

ever, never, before, always, so far, once, twice, just, already, yet

- for actions which started in the past and continue up to the present.
  I have had this computer for six months.
  Mary has been here since nine o'clock.

Time Expressions

how long, for, since

- We form the **Present Perfect Simple** with **have/has** and the **past participle** of the verb. The past participle of **regular verbs** is formed in the same way as the **Past Simple** (by adding the ending **-ed** to the verb). Each **irregular verb** forms the past participle in a different way. You can find these in the Table of Irregular Verbs on pages 152 - 153.

Affirmative		Negative	
FULL FORMS	SHORT FORMS	FULL FORMS	SHORT FORMS
I have played	I've played	I have not played	I haven't played
You have played	You've played	You have not played	You haven't played
He has played	He's played	He has not played	He hasn't played
She has played	She's played	She has not played	She hasn't played
It has played	It's played	It has not played	It hasn't played
We have played	We've played	We have not played	We haven't played
You have played	You've played	You have not played	You haven't played
They have played	They've played	They have not played	They haven't played

Interrogative	Short Answers	
Have I played?	Yes, I have.	No, I haven't.
Have you played?	Yes, you have.	No, you haven't.
Has he played?	Yes, he has.	No, he hasn't.
Has she played?	Yes, she has.	No, she hasn't.
Has it played?	Yes, it has.	No, it hasn't.
Have we played?	Yes, we have.	No, we haven't.
Have you played?	Yes, you have.	No, you haven't.
Have they played?	Yes, they have.	No, they haven't.

Time Expressions

- **ever** is used in questions.
  Have you ever played squash?
- **never** is used in affirmative sentences, but with a negative meaning.
  She's never travelled abroad.
- **already** is used in affirmative sentences and questions. It is placed between **have/has** and the past participle, or at the end of the sentence.
  He has already finished. / He has finished already.
  Has he already finished? / Has he finished already?
- **yet** is used in questions and negative sentences. It is placed at the end of the sentence.
  He hasn't finished yet.
  Has he finished yet?
- **how long** is used when asking about the duration of an action.
  How long have you known Peter?
- **for** refers to the duration of an action.
  We have known Peter for seven months.
- **since** refers to the starting point of an action (the time when the action started).
  We have known Peter since last March.

Notes:
- **have/has gone** means that someone has gone somewhere and is still there.
  have/has been means that someone has gone somewhere but has returned.
  I think Sue has gone to the airport. (She's still there.)
  Sue has been to Paris. (Now she's back.)

activities

a Complete the blanks with the Present Perfect Simple of the verbs in brackets.

1 I *have seen* (see) that film before.
2 We ________________ (read) three English books in class so far.
3 My mother ________________ (be) to London twice this year.
4 John ________________ (borrow) four CDs from me.
5 The children ________________ (eat) breakfast already and are ready to go to school.
6 You ________________ (drink) all the coffee!
7 Be quiet! The film ________________ (start).
8 My parents ________________ (have) this house since 1950.

b Circle the correct words.

1 Have you (ever) / **never** visited France?
2 My sister is a little scared because she hasn't flown **already** / **before**.
3 I have **always** / **ever** wanted to buy a house in the country.
4 We have done three exercises **so far** / **yet**.
5 Tom hasn't bought any new clothes **for** / **since** six months.
6 I have **been** / **gone** to Italy twice and I want to go there again.
7 I have **ever** / **just** heard the good news and I'm very pleased.
8 I'm sorry, Paul isn't here. He has **been** / **gone** to the cinema.

c Look at the pictures and the prompts and write questions and answers. Use the Present Perfect Simple.

1 Vera / paint / the walls / her room / blue /?

Has Vera painted the walls in her room blue?

No, she hasn't. She has painted them white.

2 Dennis / cook / chicken / yet /?

____

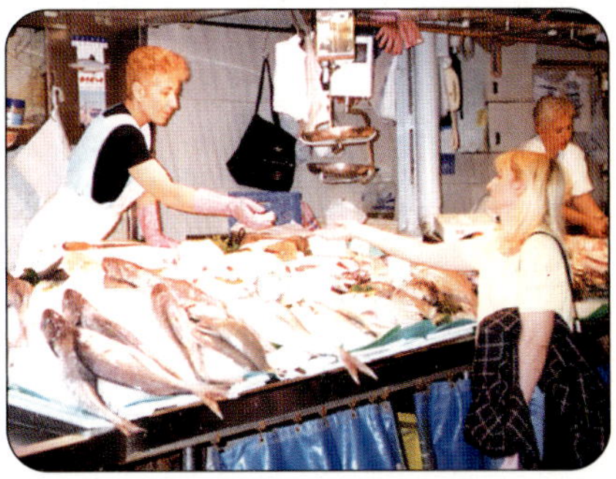

3 Mrs Peterson / just / buy / meat / ?

____

4 Sue / just / make / coffee / ?

____

5 your sisters / ever / be / Rome /?

____

6 Tom and Mary /ever / try / skiing / ?

____

d **Read the prompts below and write sentences. Use the Present Perfect Simple and for or since.**

1 Agnes / be / teacher / ten years
Agnes has been a teacher for ten years.

2 Paul / have / his dog / last month
____

3 Michael / not smoke / last summer
____

4 I / not see / Helen / two days
____

5 Mr Sullivan / be / here / 10.30
____

6 My brothers / not play / tennis / three weeks
____

e **Look at the list of things Michael wants to do today. What has he already done and what hasn't he done yet? Write sentences.**

Things to do today
- finish my history project ✓
- tell Bob about the football game on Friday ✓
- read the sports page in the newspaper ✓
- write a letter to my penfriend in India
- do my maths homework
- clean my room

1 *He has already finished his history project.*
2 ______________________________
3 ______________________________
4 ______________________________
5 ______________________________
6 ______________________________

f can you remember?

Read the text below and complete the blanks. Use the words in the box.

has ~~never~~ yet before since who which for have myself

I'm going on holiday to Peru next week. I have (**1**) *never* been to South America (**2**) __________ and I'm really excited. My sister (**3**) __________ given me some books about the history of the Incas, but I haven't read them (**4**) __________ . Anyway, I'll probably read them on the plane. It's a long flight!

I'm going to spend three weeks in Peru and I'm going to stay with my cousins (**5**) __________ have lived there (**6**) __________ 1988. They live on a farm in the mountains and I must go there by (**7**) __________ . They (**8**) __________ sent me a map with a letter (**9**) __________ explains how to get there. I hope that I won't get lost and that the people there will speak some English. You see my Spanish is poor because I haven't used it (**10**) ______________ a long time.

g Communication

Work in pairs.You and your partner are going camping for the weekend. Before you leave, you must do everything on the list below. Read the list and tick four things that you have done, but don't tell your partner. Ask and answer questions to find out how many things you have both done. Then, read the results. Are you ready to go?

vocabulary box

pack
tent
sleeping bag
engine
tinned food
fishing equipment
first aid kit

e.g. **A :** *Have you found the tent?*
B : *Yes, I have. / No, I haven't.*

- find tent ☐
- pack sleeping bags ☐
- check car engine ☐
- buy tinned food and bottles of water ☐
- pack fishing equipment ☐
- pack first aid kit ☐
- buy film for camera ☐
- put everything in car ☐

Are you ready to go?

If you have done everything on the list: You are ready to go.

If you have done 6-7 things on the list: You are almost ready to go.

If you have done only 4-5 things on the list: You aren't ready to go.

h writing

What are some exciting things that you and your best friend have done? Write a few sentences.

....

....

....

....

....

Unit 11

Present Perfect Simple vs. Past Simple
The verb *used to*

Have you heard of cliff-diving?

Read the text below.

Look out below!

Ray Thompson was in Acapulco, Mexico, last week for the cliff-diving competition. There, he **met** Jodie Stone, a female cliff-diver.

- **Have you always wanted to be a cliff-diver?**
  Not really. I **used to** do lots of different things when I **was** younger, like dancing, rock climbing, bungee-jumping…
- **How long have you been a cliff-diver?**
  For several years. I **started** in 1994 and then in 1996 I **took part** in the competition here. That **was** the first time they **let** women take part.
- **Have you ever felt scared at the top of a cliff?**
  Well, the first time I **tried** cliff-diving I **was** a bit scared, but I **haven't felt** scared since then.
- **What's your favourite diving place?**
  I've travelled to different diving places all over the world. Last year I **went** to South Africa and it **was** fine, but I think I like Acapulco the best!

The sentences below are wrong. Rewrite them and correct them.

1 Jodie Stone still does bungee-jumping.

Jodie Stone used to do bungee-jumping when she was younger.

2 Jodie was a cliff-diver from 1994 to 1996.

____

3 Jodie has never felt scared at the top of a cliff.

____

4 Jodie travelled to different diving places last year.

____

Grammar

a Present Perfect Simple vs. Past Simple

The **Present Perfect Simple** is used:

- for actions that happened in the past but we don't mention when exactly.
  I have visited Africa.
- with the time expressions:
  ever, never, before, always, how long, so far, since, for, already, just, yet.

The **Past Simple** is used:

- for actions which happened at a specific time in the past.
  I visited Africa last summer.
- with the time expressions:
  last week/month/year, ago, yesterday, in 1990, etc.

Note:

- **ago** is always used with the **Past Simple**.
  I saw this film two weeks ago.
- **before** is used with the **Present Perfect Simple**.
  I've seen this film before.

b The verb *used to*

The verb **used to** is followed by the base form of a verb. It describes actions that happened often or regularly in the past, but they no longer happen. We form the interrogative and negative with **did/ didn't**.

Mark and I used to walk to school together.
That building used to be a school 20 years ago.
Did you use to play football when you were younger?
When he lived with us, he didn't use to smoke.

activities

a Complete the table.

Infinitive	Past Simple	Past Participle
______	broke	______
cost	______	______
______	______	done
______	______	fallen
grow	______	______
______	learnt	______
______	put	______
______	______	shown
steal	______	______

b **Complete the sentences below. Use used to and the prompts given.**

1 Paula ___*used to be very fat*___ but she has lost a lot of weight. (very fat)

2 Jason ______________________ but now he drinks only tea or milk. (lots of coffee)

3 My sister is a quiet girl but she ______________________ when she was younger. (noisy)

4 The Hills ______________________ but now they have only got a canary. (four cats, two dogs)

5 We ______________________ when we lived in Italy, but we never eat any now. (a lot of spaghetti)

6 I ______________________ when I was younger, but now I prefer playing tennis. (football)

c **Read the dialogues and circle the correct words.**

1 **Teacher:** **Have you finished** / **Did you finish** your projects yet?
Mark: I have. I **have finished** / **finished** it yesterday.
Teacher: Good, then you can bring it to class tomorrow.

2 **Michelle:** **Did you ever be** / **Have you ever been** to London?
Luise: No, I **never travelled** / **have never travelled** to England. What about you?
Michelle: I **have gone** / **went** to London with my cousin last year. We **stayed** / **have stayed** there for two weeks and **have studied** / **studied** English at a language school.

3 **Bob:** Let's go to the swimming pool.
John: I can't, I **just woken up** / **have just woken up** and I **haven't had** / **didn't have** breakfast yet.
Bob: But it's noon! What time **did you go** / **have you gone** to bed last night?

d **This is Tom's diary for the weekend. Imagine it's Sunday noon now and answer the questions below. If the answer is yes, write when it happened.**

My Weekend

Saturday	Sunday
buy computer game (morning)	wash car (morning)
write letter to penfriend (afternoon)	take dog for walk (afternoon)
visit Sarah (evening)	give Helen her book (evening)

1 Has he bought a computer game?

Yes, he has. He bought it on Saturday morning.

2 Has he taken the dog for a walk?

____

3 Has he visited Sarah?

____

4 Has he washed the car?

____

5 Has he given Helen her book back?

____

6 Has he written a letter to his penfriend?

____

e **Complete the blanks with the Past Simple or the Present Perfect Simple of the verbs in brackets.**

Since 1998 my family and I *have spent* (spend) all our summer holidays abroad. In 1998 we ____________ (visit) Spain and in 1999 we ____________ (go) to Germany. We ____________ (be) to five different countries so far; Spain, Germany, Egypt, Greece and Poland. We are now on holiday in Italy. We ____________ (arrive) in Rome two days ago. Yesterday our tour guide ____________ (take) us on a tour of the city and we ____________ (see) the Colosseum and many other interesting places. Tomorrow we're going to Naples. I'm excited because I ____________ (always want) to see Mt. Vesuvius. After that we're going north to Florence or Venice, but we ____________ (not decide) where yet.

f **can you remember?**

There is one mistake in each of the sentences below. Find it and correct it.

1 Neil ~~has written~~ *wrote* a letter to Fiona yesterday.

2 I haven't seen Andrew since three weeks.

3 The ancient Greeks use to build walls around their cities.

4 Sally didn't do her homework yet.

5 I haven't never travelled by plane.

6 The Smiths bought their house three years before.

7 Bob has rang you three times, please call him back.

8 When I was younger I used to walking to work.

g Communication

Work in pairs.

Student A Go to page 139

Student B Go to page 147

vocabulary box

advertise
hire
decorate
invite
put up

h writing

Write a few sentences about the places in the pictures. Answer the questions below.

Have you ever been to any of these places?
When did you go there?
Who did you go with?
What did you do there?
Did you enjoy yourself?

circus

amusement park

zoo

Unit 12

Present Perfect Progressive

How long have people been skiing?

Read the text below.

Stone Age Skiers

Skiing has been a sport since the early 19th century, but people **haven't been skiing** for only 200 years. Believe it or not, people **have been using** skis for thousands of years!

Eric Peterson is an archaeologist who **has been working** on a project in Scandinavia for the last three years. He told us: "In Norway we have found rock pictures of people on skis which are over 5,000 years old. In Sweden we have found a 4,500-year-old ski. Of course, Stone Age people didn't ski for fun. They used skis to travel from one place to another."

Complete the sentences below with the words in the box. You will use some words twice.

been	for	five	have	hundred	skiing	thousand	two	using

1 People ________ ________ ________ for fun ________ about ________ ________ years.

2 People ________ ________ ________ skis ________ about ________ ________ years.

Grammar

Present Perfect Progressive

We use the **Present Perfect Progressive**:

- for repeated actions or for situations which started in the past and continue up to the present, regularly or uniterrupted.

  How long have you been living here?
  He has been working in this shop since 1998.
  I have been waiting for you for twenty minutes.
  She has been writing letters all morning.

Time Expressions
how long, for, since
all morning/day/night, etc.

- for actions which were happening over a period of time in the past and may or may not have finished, but their results are obvious in the present.

  Ted has been working hard and he is very tired.

- We form the **Present Perfect Progressive** with the Present Perfect Simple of the verb *be* (**subject + have/has been**) and the main verb with the ending **-ing**.

Affirmative		Negative	
FULL FORMS	SHORT FORMS	FULL FORMS	SHORT FORMS
I have been playing	I've been playing	I have not been playing	I haven't been playing
You have been playing	You've been playing	You have not been playing	You haven't been playing
He has been playing	He's been playing	He has not been playing	He hasn't been playing
She has been playing	She's been playing	She has not been playing	She hasn't been playing
It has been playing	It's been playing	It has not been playing	It hasn't been playing
We have been playing	We've been playing	We have not been playing	We haven't been playing
You have been playing	You've been playing	You have not been playing	You haven't been playing
They have been playing	They've been playing	They have not been playing	They haven't been playing

Interrogative	Short Answers	
Have I been playing?	Yes, I have.	No, I haven't.
Have you been playing?	Yes, you have.	No, you haven't.
Has he been playing?	Yes, he has.	No, he hasn't.
Has she been playing?	Yes, she has.	No, she hasn't.
Has it been playing?	Yes, it has.	No, it hasn't.
Have we been playing?	Yes, we have.	No, we haven't.
Have you been playing?	Yes, you have.	No, you haven't.
Have they been playing?	Yes, they have.	No, they haven't.

Notes:

- The **Present Perfect Simple** emphasises the result of an action. The **Present Perfect Progressive** emphasises the duration of an action.

  I have done all my grammar exercises.
  I have been doing grammar exercises all afternoon.

- **Stative verbs** are not normally used in the **Present Perfect Progressive**.

activities

a **Complete the blanks with the Present Perfect Progressive of the verbs in the box.**

work	~~walk~~	talk	play	wait	watch

1 **Mother:** Why are you so wet?
Penny: I ___*have been walking*___ in the rain.

2 **Father:** How did the boys get so dirty?
Mother: They ______________________ football all afternoon.

3 **George:** What will we have for dinner?
Carol: We'll get some pizza because I ______________________ all day and I haven't had time to cook.

4 **Father:** Why are Tom's eyes so red?
Mother: He ______________________ TV for hours.

5 **Father:** Why hasn't Kelly finished her homework yet?
Mother: She ______________________ on the telephone all afternoon.

6 **Jenny:** Where's the bus?
John: I don't know. We ______________________ for it for half an hour now.

b **Complete the blanks in the sentences with the Present Perfect Progressive of the verbs in brackets and for or since.**

1 Mrs Roberts ___*has been teaching*___ (teach) at our school __________ twenty years.
2 My grandfather ______________________ (collect) stamps __________ 1962.
3 The soldiers ______________________ (fight) __________ two days.
4 Donna ______________________ (clean) her room __________ 9 o'clock.
5 Bob ______________________ (write) letters __________ early this morning.
6 Lisa and Tom ______________________ (learn) German __________ three years.
7 The children______________________ (sleep) __________ nine hours.
8 Mr Collins ______________________ (grow) vegetables in his garden __________ last year.

c Look at the pictures and the prompts and write questions and answers. Use the Present Perfect Progressive.

1 Mary / play / computer games / afternoon / ?

Has Mary been playing computer games all afternoon?

No, she hasn't. She has been repairing her bicycle.

2 Michael / read / comic books / morning / ?

___

___

___

___

3 your sister / iron / afternoon / ?

___

___

___

___

4 Rob and Emma / send / e-mails / evening / ?

___

___

___

___

5 the girls / shop / day / ?

___

___

___

___

6 Beth's father / work / night / ?

___

___

___

___

d Complete the text with the Present Perfect Simple or the Present Perfect Progressive of the verbs in brackets.

Everybody in the Patterson family (**1**) *has been* (be) very busy today because they (**2**) ________________ (get) ready to celebrate Mr Patterson's birthday. Mrs Patterson (**3**) ________________ (cook) all morning. So far, she (**4**) ________________ (make) two cakes, a pie and lots of biscuits. Her daughter, Tina, (**5**) ________________ (clean) the house. Tina (**6**) ________________ (clean) the living room already, but she (**7**) ________________ (not clean) the dining room yet. Tina's brothers, Bill and Ted, (**8**) ________________ (do) the shopping, but they (**9**) ________________ (not finish) yet. They (**10**) ________________ (buy) all the drinks and they (**11**) ________________ (be) to the greengrocer's. They (**12**) ________________ (not be) to the butcher's yet. Mr Patterson (**13**) ________________ (work) in the garden and he (**14**) ________________ (just, finish). He (**15**) ________________ (prepare) everything for the barbecue.

e can you remember?

Choose *a*, *b* or *c*.

1 The students have *been doing* their homework all evening.
a. doing **(b.)** been doing **c.** be doing

2 Kate has ____________ in the USA for ten years.
a. living **b.** been lived **c.** been living

3 Tom is very tired because he has ____________ for four hours.
a. driving **b.** been driven **c.** been driving

4 Marta has never ____________ to England.
a. travelling **b.** travelled **c.** been travelling

5 My brother ____________ the car yesterday.
a. fixed **b.** has fixed **c.** has been fixing

6 How ____________ has he been waiting here?
a. much **b.** time **c.** long

7 Baby Linda is ill, she ____________ all night.
a. is crying **b.** has cried **c.** has been crying

8 I have been calling James ____________ 8.00 am but he hasn't answered the phone.
a. for **b.** at **c.** since

9 David ____________ all his homework last night.
a. did **b.** has done **c.** has been doing

10 Tom isn't here; he has ____________ to the cinema with his friends.
a. been **b.** gone **c.** been going

f Communication

Work in pairs.
Ask each other questions using the ideas below. Then, ask how long you have been doing these activities. Use words from the vocabulary box.

vocabulary box

collect stamps/coins	water-polo
make model planes	table tennis
do jigsaw puzzles	hockey
play board games	cricket

What / be / hobbies / ? What / sports / play / ? What / foreign languages / learn / at present / ?

e.g.
A : *What are your hobbies?*
B : *I ...*
A : *How long have you been ...?*
B : *I have been ... for ... / since ...*

g writing

Imagine that you're having a party tonight. Write a few sentences about what you and the members of your family have been doing all day and what you have done so far.

....

....

....

....

....

Unit 13

Can, Could
Be able to
May, Might
Shall

At the airport

Look at the picture and read the speech bubbles.

Now complete the speech bubbles with can, can't or may.

Grammar

Can, **could**, **may**, **might** and **shall** are **modal verbs** and:
- They do not form all the tenses.
- They are the same in all persons, singular and plural.
- They form the interrogative and negative without auxiliary verbs (do/did).
- They followed by the base form of a verb, without to.

a Can

I can draw. *Can you draw?* *She cannot/can't draw.*

We use **can**:

- to express **ability** in the present. *The baby can walk.*
- to **request** something. *Can you close the window, please?*
- to express **possibility**. *Snow can be dangerous for drivers.*
- to **ask for, give** or **refuse permission**. *Can I leave the room? Yes, you can. / No, you can't.*

b Could

I could swim. *Could you swim?* *He could not/couldn't swim.*

We use **could**:

- to express **ability** in the past. *I could climb trees when I was young.*
- to **request** something. *Could you help me with my homework, please?*
- to express **possibility**. *Mary could come tonight.*
- to **ask for permission**. *Could I borrow your pen?*

Note: It is more polite to use **could** instead of **can** in **requests** and when **asking for permission**.

Be able to

Be able to expresses **ability** and forms all tenses. It is mainly used in tenses where we cannot use **can** (e.g. Future, Present Perfect, etc.).
He'll be able to play football on Saturday. *I haven't been able to talk to him yet.*

c May

He may watch TV. *May I watch TV?* *They may not watch TV.*

We use **may**:

- to express **possibility** in the present or future. *He may be at home.*
- to **ask for**, **give** or **refuse permission**. *May I go out? Yes, you may. / No, you may not.*

Note: It is more polite to use **may** instead of **can** when **asking for permission**.

d Might

He might be out. *Might she be out?* *They might not be out.*

We use **might**:

- to express **slight possibility** in the present or future. *He might be at work.*

e Shall

We use **shall**:

- only with *I* and *we* in the interrogative.
- when we **offer** to do something. — *Shall I open the window?*
- to **suggest** something. — *Shall we go to the cinema?*

activities

a Read the chart below and write sentences about the people. Use can, could and will be able to.

	five years ago	now	in five years
Kelly – play piano		✗	✓
Kevin and John – dive	✗	✓	
Richard – play chess well	✗	✓	
Tom and Sarah – ride bicycle		✗	✓
Linda – fly plane	✗	✓	
Eddie and Marianne - use computer		✗	✓

1 *Kelly can't play the piano now but she will be able to play the piano in five years.*

2 ____________________

3 ____________________

4 ____________________

5 ____________________

6 ____________________

b Read the situations below and write questions asking for permission. Use can, could, may.

1 Kate wants to leave school early today. What does she ask her teacher?

Could/May I leave school early today?

2 Bob and Jeff want to go to the beach tomorrow. What do they ask their parents?

____

3 You are in a shop and you want to try on a shirt. What do you ask the shop assistant?

____

4 You are at your friend's house and you want to use the phone. What do you ask him?

____

5 George wants to borrow his sister's CD player. What does he ask her?

____

6 Carol and John haven't finished their project yet and they want to bring it to school on Monday. What do they ask their teacher?

____

c **Look at the pictures and the prompts and write sentences expressing possibility. Use may, might or could.**

1 Danny / go swimming

Danny may/might/could go swimming.

2 Tony / buy

____

3 it / rain

____

4 Mr Asher / catch

____

5 Philip / win

____

6 Susan / take

____

d **Look at the pictures and the prompts and write requests. Use can or could.**

1 close / window

Can/Could you close the window, please?

2 give / pencil

____

3 open / door

____

4 feed / dog

5 lift / sofa

6 answer / phone

e **Read the situations. What would you say in each case? Write a question for each one. Use shall and the prompts in the box.**

go / beach	play / board game	carry / books	help	buy / shirt	~~turn on / light~~

1 You and your brother are in your room. It's dark and you can't read.
Shall I turn on the light?

2 It is hot and you and your friends don't know where to go.

3 Your sister is having trouble with her homework.

4 It's your father's birthday. You and your brother don't know what to buy him.

5 Your friend is going to the library. He is carrying twelve big books.

6 You are at home with two friends. It's raining and you don't know what to do.

f can you remember?

Circle the correct words.

1 Cathy is a very good singer and she **can dance** / **couldn't dance** very well, too.

2 I'm very sorry, but I **won't be able to come** / **haven't come** to your party on Saturday.

3 My brother **might go** / **used to go** to the cinema every week when he was a student.

4 **Have you already finished** / **Did you already finish** the exercise?

5 Take your jacket with you. It **might get** / **will be able to get** cold in the evening.

6 George has always loved sports. He **can swim** / **could swim** when he was three years old!

7 We **have visited / visited** the Museum of Natural History yesterday.

8 **Could you tell me / May you tell me** the time, please?

9 It's very hot in this room. **Did I use to / Shall I** open the window?

10 We **haven't seen / may not see** Julie since September.

11 Charlie **used to go / might go** on holiday to Mexico this summer.

12 Diane **played / has played** hockey before.

g Communication

Work in two groups.

- Group A: Imagine you're in the classroom and then at the zoo.
- Group B: Imagine you're in a shop and then at a restaurant.
- Each group thinks of at least four questions for each situation, asking for permission or making requests. Use words and ideas from the vocabulary box.
- The winner is the group which has formed the most correct questions.

vocabulary box

ZOO	SHOP	RESTAURANT
penguin	try on	menu
kangaroo	show	plate
insect house	changing room	fork
reptile house		spoon

e.g. **A:** *I'm in the classroom. May I go out?*
I'm at the zoo. Can I touch the snake?
B: *I'm in a shop. Could I see that T-shirt?*
I'm at a restaurant. May I have a glass of water, please?

h writing

Complete the chart below about yourself. Tick (✓) the things you could do three years ago, the things you can do now and what you will be able to do in three years. Then, write a few sentences.

	three years ago	now	in three years
speak English			
drive a car			
play basketball			
ski			
paint well			

....

....

....

....

....

....

Unit 14

Infinitive
-ing form
Too / Enough

An exciting sport

Read the text below.

Do you enjoy doing water sports?

Would you like to try something different?

Then canoeing might be the sport for you!

- Join the local canoeing club and try out this exciting sport.
- It's a sport for all ages. Nobody's **too old to try**.
- You won't need many lessons before you are **good enough to go** out on your own.

SAFETY FIRST

Wear a helmet **to protect** your head and a wet suit **to keep warm**. You can **hire** a canoe, a helmet and a wet suit at the canoeing club.

Which of the following sentences is true for you? Tick the appropriate box.

- I'd love **to learn** more about this sport. ☐
- I don't mind **trying** this sport. ☐
- I'm not interested in **trying** this sport. ☐

Grammar

a Infinitive

There are two types of **infinitive**:
- **full infinitive**: **to** + base form of verb — *to go*
- **bare infinitive**: base form of verb without **to** — *play*

We use the **full infinitive**:

- after the verbs **want**, **would like**, **would love**, **decide**, **hope**, **manage**, **try**, etc.
  I've decided to study in England. *I'd like to tell you something.*
- to express **purpose**.
  She called to tell me the news.

We use the **bare infinitive**:

- after modal verbs: **can**, **could**, **may**, **might**, **must**, **shall**, etc. *She can ride a bike.*

b -ing form

The **-ing form** (base form of the verb + -ing) can be used as a noun.

We use **-ing forms**:

- as subjects of verbs. *Eating junk food is bad for your health.*
- after the verbs **like**, **love**, **hate**, **enjoy**, **prefer**, **don't mind**, **continue**, **can't stand**, **stop**, **finish**, **start**, etc. *I don't mind working late.*
- after prepositions. *I use this knife for cutting bread.*
- after the verb **go**, to indicate activities (**go shopping, go swimming, go camping**, etc.).

c Too / Enough

Too

- It is means "more than necessary". It has a negative meaning.
- It is used before adjectives and adverbs and it is often followed by a **full infinitive**.
  This coffee is too hot. I can't drink it. *Jeremy is too young to drive.*

Enough

- It means "adequate" or "adequately". It has a positive meaning.
- It is used after adjectives and adverbs, and before nouns, and it is often followed by a **full infinitive**.
  Jim is tall enough to reach that shelf. *I've got enough money to buy a magazine.*

activities

a Circle the correct words.

1 John: I might (go) / **to go** to the basketball game tomorrow.
Ted: I would like **see** / **to see** that game, too.
John: OK. We can **go** / **to go** together.

2 Mary: I hope **pass** / **to pass** the chemistry exam with a B.
Tina: Oh, I'm sure you will manage **to get** / **get** a B.

Mary: Well, I have studied really hard!
Tina: Then you might **get** / **to get** an A!

3 **Carol:** I want **have** / **to have** pizza for dinner tonight.
Kevin: We could **make** / **to make** pizza ourselves.
Carol: No, we haven't got any cheese. I'll go to the Pizza House **buy** / **to buy** one.

4 **Kate:** I have decided **travel** / **to travel** to England this summer.
Lisa: England? Where exactly?
Kate: I'm going to London **visit** / **to visit** the Tate Gallery. There are some beautiful paintings there and I would love **see** / **to see** them. Then I may **go** / **to go** to Kent.

b Answer the questions below as in the example. Use the prompts in the boxes.

watch / film | make / cake | go / jogging | tell / news | ~~swim / in~~ sea | buy / present for Mark

1 Why did Harry go to the beach?
He went to the beach to swim in the sea.

2 Why did Marge go to the cinema?
____

3 Why did Brian ring Kathy?
____

4 Why did Diane put on her trainers?
____

5 Why did Fiona buy some eggs?
____

6 Why did Henry go shopping?
____

c Complete the sentences with the –ing form of the verbs in the box.

paint | drive | do | collect | exercise | ~~buy~~

1 Adam is thinking about *buying* a new computer.

2 __________ stamps is Jeff's favourite hobby.

3 I use these brushes for __________ pictures.

4 __________ a big car is not a problem for Laura.

5 __________ is good for your health.

6 David isn't very good at __________ jigsaw puzzles.

d Look at the table and write sentences about Fred. Use the –ing form.

	can't stand	don't mind	like	enjoy	love	interested in
clean room	✓					
do homework		✓				
play tennis				✓		
watch TV			✓			
learn about other countries						✓
listen to music					✓	

1 *Fred can't stand cleaning his room.*

2 ______________________

3 ______________________

4 ______________________

5 ______________________

6 ______________________

e Look at the pictures and the prompts and write sentences. Use too or enough.

hot

1 Jack can't eat his soup.

It's too hot.

fast

2 Sally can win the race.

____

difficult

3 Molly can't do this exercise.

____

money

4 Carl can buy this CD.

____

rich

5 The Jones can't buy this house.

____

sugar

6 Susie can't make a cake.

____

f Rewrite the sentences below. Use the adjectives in the box and too or enough.

warm	weak	dirty	young	~~tall~~

1 Michael is too short to play basketball well.

Michael isn't tall enough to play basketball well.

2 Bruce isn't old enough to drive a car.

____

3 It's too cold to go swimming.

____

4 This jacket isn't clean enough to wear.

____

5 Mary isn't strong enough to lift that box.

____

g can you remember?

Read the text and circle the correct words.

When Eric was eight years old, he wanted (**1**) **learn / to learn** how to play a musical instrument. However, his parents thought that he was (**2**) **too young / young enough**. So, he started (**3**) **have/ having** guitar lessons when he was twelve. A few years later, Eric (**4**) **can / could** play (**5**) **well enough / enough well**, and decided (**6**) **starting / to start** a rock group with some friends. They enjoyed (**7**) **play / playing** music together and they didn't mind (**8**) **to practise / practising** during most of their free time. They managed (**9**) **to become / becoming** a very good group and they played at many High School dances. When Eric went to university, he (**10**) **wasn't able to / can't** play with his friends because he didn't have (**11**) **enough time / time enough**. Now he has finished university and he says that he might (**12**) **try / to try** to bring the group back together. Who knows? Eric (**13**) **is able to / may** become famous in the future!

h Communication

Work in pairs.

Student A Go to page 140

Student B Go to page 148

vocabulary box

go sightseeing	cruise
go hiking	trip
go horseback riding	tour
organise	helicopter
taste	

i writing

Imagine you are writing a letter to a penfriend. Tell him/her about the things that you like, the things that you don't like and what you would like to do in the future. Use the verbs in the box.

hate	can't stand	don't mind	like	enjoy	manage	want	would like

....

....

....

....

....

....

Revision Units 10-14

a **Write what the people used to do. Use the prompts in the box.**

~~play / guitar~~	catch / bus	write / letters	eat / sweets	grow / vegetables	watch / TV

1 Billy *used to play the guitar* but now he plays the piano.
2 I ____________ to my friends but now I send them e-mails.
3 Jenny ____________ to work, but now she drives her car.
4 David ____________ but now he buys them from the greengrocer's.
5 Karen ____________ but now she doesn't because she wants to lose weight.
6 Andy ____________ in the evenings but now he reads books.

b **Complete the blanks with the Present Perfect Simple of the verbs in the brackets.**

1 **Peter:** Is everything ready for the barbecue on Sunday?
Helen: Well, there are a few things that I (**1**) *haven't done* (not do) yet.
Peter: (**2**) ____________ (you / be) to the butcher's to get the meat?
Helen: Yes, I have, and Carl (**3**) ____________ (already / borrow) some chairs from our neighbour, but I (**4**) ____________ (not buy) the drinks yet.

2 **Brian:** I'm very excited about tomorrow's game. I hope we win.
Stuart: Don't worry. Your team (**5**) ____________ (not lose) a game this year.
Brian: Isn't it great? We (**6**) ____________ (win) fifteen games so far.
Stuart: How many goals (**7**) ____________ (you / score)?
Brian: I (**8**) ____________ (score) eleven goals.

c **Complete the blanks with the Present Perfect Simple or the Past Simple of the verbs in brackets.**

Mrs Carlyle (**1**) *has been* (be) a photographer for many years and she has got lots of cameras. She (**2**) ____________ (have) her oldest camera for thirty years. She (**3**) ____________ (buy) it when she (**4**) ____________ (be) seventeen and it's her favourite one. She (**5**) ____________ (take) many pictures with it.

Mrs Carlyle (**6**) ____________ (travel) to many places to take pictures. Next week she's going to Mexico. She (**7**) ____________ (never / visit) Mexico before, but she (**8**) ____________ (be) to the USA. She (**9**) ____________ (go) to New York two years ago. She (**10**) ____________ (make) lots of friends there, but she (**11**) ____________ (see) them since then.

d Look at the pictures and the prompts below and write sentences. Use the Present Perfect Progressive and for or since.

1 Anna is busy.
clean / room / 5:00
She has been cleaning her room since five o'clock.

2 Tom is angry.
wait / friends / one hour

___

3 Kim is tired.
work / 8:00 / morning

___

4 John has got a headache.
watch TV / four hours

___

5 The children are very happy.
play / park / 10:00

___

6 Steve's arms hurt.
fly / kite / two hours

___

e Read the situations and write a sentence or a question. Use can, could, may, might or shall.

1 You're very busy and you don't have time to feed the dog. What do you ask your sister?
Can / Could you feed the dog?

2 You want to visit the zoo with your friends. What do you ask your parents?

___

3 Your sister is having a shower and her mobile phone is ringing. What do you offer to do?

___

4 Your brother was telling you about a film he wanted to see at the cinema. He isn't at home now and your mother is looking for him. What do you say to her?

___

5 You and your friend are at home and you don't know what to do. You have some new CDs. What do you suggest?

___

6 You are at a restaurant and you want a glass of water. What do you ask the waiter?

___

f Circle the correct words.

1 (**Can**) / **May** you ride a bicycle?

2 My daughter **can** / **could** walk when she was only eleven months old.

3 **Shall** / **May** I have some more tea, please?

4 Ann's sister **can** / **could** climb trees easily when she was younger but she **may not** / **can't** do that now.

5 **Could** / **May** you tell me the time, please?

6 Barbara **may** / **can** play the piano very well.

7 **Shall** / **Might** I bring you some cake?

8 David won't **can** / **be able to** play football tomorrow.

g Circle the correct words.

1 In my free time I like **read** / **reading** but my brother enjoys **to play** / **playing** computer games.

2 Sally would like **to go** / **going** to university.

3 The children want to go **camp** / **camping** next weekend, but it may **rain** / **to rain**.

4 I can't stand **to iron** / **ironing**. Could you **help** / **to help** me?

5 Harry managed **to buy** / **buying** a car this year. I hope **buy** / **to buy** one next year.

6 Donna is thinking about **go** / **going** to Spain **learn** / **to learn** Spanish.

h Rewrite the sentences below using the words in brackets.

1 Roxanne isn't very tall, so she can't become a model. (enough)

Roxanne isn't tall enough to become a model.

2 Karen is quite good and can win the competition. (enough)

____

3 Tina is very tired and can't go to the cinema tonight. (too)

____

4 Joe is still very young and can't drive a car. (too)

____

5 Sue needs two stamps to send the letter, but she's got only one. (enough)

____

6 The painting is very expensive and I can't buy it. (too)

____

Unit 15

Future *Will*
Future *Going to*
Time Clauses

I'll sleep a bit longer

Read the speech bubble and the note in the picture.

What will happen next? Use will or won't and the prompts below to write sentences.

1 Neal / sleep / longer

____

2 Neal / have / big breakfast

____

3 Kate / be / angry / when / come / home

____

4 Neal / be / in trouble

____

Grammar

a Future *Will*

We use the **Future *Will***:

- for **spontaneous decisions** that we make at the moment of speaking.
  I don't like this bag. I won't buy it.
- for **promises**.
  OK, Mum. I won't do it again.
- for **warnings** and **threats**.
  Be quiet or I'll tell your mum.
- for **predictions**, usually with **perhaps** or with the verbs **think**, **believe**, **hope**, etc.
  I think he'll pass the test.
  I hope she will come on time.

Time Expressions

tomorrow/tonight
next month/year/week/Tuesday, etc.
this weekend/week/month, etc.
in an hour/year, etc.
soon

Affirmative		Negative	
FULL FORMS	SHORT FORMS	FULL FORMS	SHORT FORMS
I will go	I'll go	I will not go	I won't go
He/She/It will go	He/She/It'll go	He/She/It will not go	He/She/It won't go
We/You/They will go	We/You/They'll go	We/You/They will not go	We/You/They won't go

Interrogative	Short Answers	
Will I go?	Yes, I will.	No, I won't.
Will he/she/it go?	Yes, he/she/it will.	No, he/she/it won't.
Will we/you/they go?	Yes, we/you/they will.	No, we/you/they won't.

b Future *Going to*

We use the **Future *Going to***:

- for actions that we intend to do in the future.
  I'm going to study Biology next year.
- for predictions based on evidence.
  Look at that car! It's going to crash.

Time expressions

tomorrow/tonight
next month/year/week/Tuesday, etc.
this weekend/week/month, etc.
in an hour/year, etc.
soon

Affirmative	
FULL FORMS	SHORT FORMS
I am going to work	I'm going to work
He/She/It is going to work	He/She/It's going to work
We/You/They are going to work	We/You/They 're going to work

Negative	
FULL FORMS	SHORT FORMS
I am not going to work	I'm not going to work
He/She/It is not going to work	He/She/It isn't going to work
We/You/They are not going to work	We/You/They aren't going to work

Interrogative	Short Answers	
Am I going to work?	Yes, I am.	No, I'm not.
Is he/she/it going to work?	Yes, he/she/it is.	No, he/she/it isn't.
Are we/you/they going to work?	Yes, we/you/they are.	No, we/you/they aren't.

Note: We use the **Present Progressive** for actions that we have planned to do in the near future (we mention the time).

I'm visiting my grandparents tonight.

C Time Clauses

Time clauses define when the action described in the main clause takes place. Time clauses begin with the words **when**, **after**, **before** and **until**. When a **time clause** refers to the future, the verb that it contains is in the **Present Simple** and the verb in the **main clause** is in the **Future *Will***.

Main Clause	Time Clause
I'll give you your book	when I see you tomorrow.
I'll be there	before he wakes up.
They'll call us	after the film finishes.
She'll wait	until we get back.

Notes:
- When the **time clause** comes before the **main clause**, the two are separated by a comma.
  When I see you tomorrow, I'll give you your book.
- When the **time clause** comes after the **main clause**, the two are not separated by a comma.
  I'll give you your book when I see you tomorrow.

activities

a Look at the prompts and write questions and answers. Use the Future *Will*.

1 people / live / moon / future / ?
→ Yes

Will people live on the moon in the future?

Yes, they will.

2 astronauts / travel / Mars / next year / ?
→ No

____

____

3 people / have / cars / thirty years from now / ?
→ Yes / but / electric

____

____

4 people / work / future / ?
→ Yes / but / work from home

____

____

5 children / learn / from computers / soon?
→ Yes

____

____

6 people / live / forever / future / ?
→ No / but / live / longer

____

____

b Match the sentences 1-6 with the responses a-f.

1 I really like this dress.

2 Kathy, you didn't do very well in your test.

3 I can't cook dinner, I'm too tired.

4 I'm sorry I'm late for class.

5 What will Sue do during the holidays?

6 The theatre is very far and I'm late.

a Don't worry. I'll drive you there.

b I know, I'll try to study harder.

c She'll probably go to an island.

d That's all right, we'll order something.

e I'll buy it for you.

f Don't do it again or I'll phone your parents.

c Complete the dialogue. Use the Future *Going to* of the verbs in brackets.

Peter: (**1**) *Are you going to study* (you / study) for the maths test now?

Martha: Yes, I am. My brother (**2**) __________ (help) me with some things I don't understand. What (**3**) __________ (you / do)?

Peter: I'm going swimming with George.

Martha: That's not a very good idea. Look at those clouds. It (**4**) __________ (rain).

Peter: We (**5**) __________ (not be) outside. We (**6**) __________ (swim) in the new indoor swimming pool at the sports centre.

Martha: Oh, well, the weather (**7**) __________ (not be) a problem then.

d Look at the pictures and the prompts and write sentences. Use the Future *Going to*.

enter

1 *The students are going to enter the classroom.*

jump

2 __________

play

3 __________

fall

4 __________

eat

5 __________

land

6 __________

e Complete the blanks with the Present Simple or the Future *Will* of the verbs in brackets.

1 I'll give you this book when I ___*finish*___ (finish) reading it.

2 After Keith does his homework, he ____________ (play) computer games.

3 We won't leave until Mary ____________ (arrive).

4 I will tidy my room before I ____________ (go) out on Saturday.

5 We ____________ (watch) the film when the children go to bed.

6 After we ____________ (have) lunch, we will start working on our project.

f Join the sentences below. Use the words in brackets.

1 John and I will buy a present for Mary. Then we will go to the party. (before)

John and I will buy a present for Mary before we go to the party.

2 I will read the book. Then I will return it to the library. (after)

____

3 My sisters will clean the house. Then they will decorate it. (until)

____

4 James will make breakfast. Then he will wake his sister up. (when)

____

5 Mark will call Donna. Then he will visit her. (before)

____

g can you remember?

Choose *a*, *b* or *c*.

1 Helen wants ___*to become*___ a dancer, but her parents don't like the idea.

(a.) to become **b.** become **c.** becoming

2 I ______________ drink this coffee because it's too sweet.

a. not going to **b.** won't going to **c.** am not going to

3 I haven't studied well. I hope I'll manage ______________ the test.

a. passing **b.** to pass **c.** pass

4 I enjoy walking in the park before I ______________ work.

a. will start **b.** am going to start **c.** start

5 When Mary finishes her exams, she'll go to Kent ______________ her friends.

a. to visit **b.** visit **c.** visiting

6 ______________ too many sweets is bad for your teeth.

a. To eat **b.** Eat **c.** Eating

7 Clark won't ________________ his parents' house because he can't stand living alone.

a. to leave **b.** leave **c.** leaving

8 Claire can't join the swimming team because she isn't ________________ .

a. old enough **b.** enough old **c.** too old

h Communication

Work in pairs.
What are you going to do next Saturday? Complete the diary page below. Use some of the ideas in the vocabulary box and your own. Then, ask each other questions as in the example and complete the diary page about your partner. Compare your answers.

vocabulary box

do washing-up
tidy room
go jogging

e.g. **A :** *Are you going to ...?*
B : *Yes, I am. / No, I'm not.*
A : *When are you going to ...?*
B : *I'm going to ... in the morning/afternoon/evening.*

SATURDAY

	YOU	YOUR PARTNER
morning		
afternoon		
evening		

i writing

Write a few sentences about the plans that your family and friends have made for next weekend. Use the Future *Going to*.

....

....

....

....

....

....

....

....

Unit 16

Conditional Sentences Type 1

If she answers the telephone...

Read what Bill is thinking.

If Jenny is free tonight, **I'll ask** her to come to the cinema with me. We'll have a great time. But what **if she says** no? Well, **if I ask** her nicely, **she won't** say no, I hope... **If she doesn't want** to go to the cinema, **we can go** to a fast food restaurant. I'll borrow my brother's car... But why isn't she answering the phone? **I won't be able** to ask her **unless she answers** the phone... Maybe she isn't at home. I'll ring her on her mobile... **If she doesn't answer** that, **I won't ring** her again...

Now complete what Jenny is thinking.

It is already eight o'clock. If Bill ____________ (not call) me, I ____________ (not speak) to him again...

Grammar

Conditional Sentences Type 1

- We use **Conditional Sentences Type 1** to express something which is possible to happen in the present or future.
  If I have enough money, I'll buy a computer.
- **Conditional Sentences** consist of the **if-clause** and the **main clause**.

if-clause	main clause
If + Present Simple *If you come to the party,*	**Future *Will*** *you will meet my friends.*

- When the **if-clause** is before the **main clause**, we separate the two clauses with a comma. We do not use a comma when the **if-clause** is after the **main clause**.
  If you come to the party, you'll meet my friends.
  You will meet my friends if you come to the party.
- In the **main clause**, besides **Future *Will***, we can use:
  • modal verbs **can**, **may**, **might**, **must** *If the weather is good, we may go for a picnic.*
  • **Imperative** *If you go out, take an umbrella.*
- We can use **unless** instead of **if + not**.
  I won't go to the party unless you come with me. (= I won't go to the party if you don't come with me.)

activities

a Match the if-clauses 1-8 with the main clauses a-h.

1 If Kate wants to go shopping, → **b**
2 If we take a taxi,
3 If you like Chinese food,
4 If John phones,
5 Unless it is very quiet,
6 If you aren't too busy,
7 If I'm very tired after work,
8 If Betty and Michael want to lose weight,

a tell him to call back later.
b give her some money.
c I may not go to my aerobics class.
d I'll teach you how to cook it.
e take the dog for a walk.
f they must stop eating sweets.
g my brother can't sleep.
h we won't be late.

b Complete the blanks in the dialogues with the Present Simple or the Future *Will* of the verbs in brackets.

1 **Andy:** Are you going to the concert on Saturday?
Tina: Well, I (**1**) ___*will go*___ (go) if I do well in my English test.
Andy: What (**2**) ______________ (happen) if you don't do well in the test?
Tina: If I (**3**) ______________ (not get) an A, my father (**4**) ______________ (not let) me go to the concert!

2 Sally: Mark, can I borrow your bicycle?

Mark: OK, you can have it if you (**5**) ______________ (promise) to bring it back in an hour.

Sally: I promise.

Mark: And remember. If anything happens to it, you (**6**) ______________ (take) it to the bike shop and you (**7**) ______________ (pay) to fix it, OK?

Sally: OK, OK. Now if you (**8**) ______________ (not stop) talking to me, I (**9**) ______________ (not be) back in an hour!

c Rewrite the sentences below. Use unless.

1 I won't watch the film tonight if it is not a comedy.

I won't watch the film tonight unless it is a comedy.

2 You might not pass the test if you don't study harder.

____

3 We can't go skiing if there is not enough snow.

____

4 My father won't give me any money if I don't clean the garage.

____

5 If you don't explain the problem to me, I can't help you.

____

6 If you aren't an electrician, you mustn't try to fix the TV.

____

d Read the sentences and make Conditional Sentences Type 1.

1 I must run faster to win the race.

If I run faster, I will win the race.

2 Kelly will try to finish her homework before eight o'clock. Then she may go to the cinema.

____

3 Tony wants to visit Egypt. He will see the Pyramids there.

____

4 Don't sit on that chair. It might break.

____

5 Drive carefully and you won't have an accident.

____

6 Are you very tired? Then, you must go home and relax.

____

e can you remember?

Answer the questions below.

1 What will you do when you finish your homework today?

When I finish my homework today, I'll watch TV.

2 What will you do when you get home from school tomorrow afternoon?

____

3 What will you do if your parents don't let you go out next Saturday night?

____

4 What will you do before you go to bed tonight?

____

5 What will you do after you have breakfast on Sunday?

____

f Communication

Game.
Work in two groups. Gary Mackinsky wants to go on holiday, but he hasn't decided where yet, Africa or Antarctica? One group should think about Africa and the other about Antarctica. The students in each group should use the ideas in the vocabulary box and their own to make Conditional Sentences Type 1. The group with the most correct sentences is the winner.

vocabulary box

fish	igloo
hunt	jungle
bite	wild animals
freeze	tiger
build	penguin
stay	lion
go on a safari	whale
	ice

e.g. **A:** *If Gary goes to Africa, he will see lots of wild animals.*
B: *If Gary goes to Antarctica, he will see lots of penguins.*

g writing

Write a few sentences about what you and a friend will do if the weather is good tomorrow and what you will do if it rains.

....

....

....

....

Unit 17

Question Words
Subject / Object Questions

How much do you know?

Do the quiz below. Match the questions 1-10 with the answers a-j.

1 How many eggs do British people eat every year?

2 Who played Eva Peron in the film Evita?

3 What is an ugli?

4 Where do penguins live?

5 Which of Steven Spielberg's films is about dinosaurs?

6 When did white lines first appear on roads?

7 Where do the Maori people come from?

8 How old are the Pyramids in Egypt?

9 Who did David Beckham marry in 1999?

10 What do whales usually eat?

a A fruit
b New Zealand
c In 1914
d Small fish
e Madonna
f Victoria Adams
g 10 billion
h The South Pole
i Jurassic Park
j Over 4,500 years old

1 ___ 2 ___ 3 ___ 4 ___ 5 ___ 6 ___ 7 ___ 8 ___ 9 ___ 10 ___

Grammar

a Question Words

We use **question words** at the beginning of questions, to ask for information. **Question words** are:

Who?	We ask about people.	*Who is at the door?*	*Mary.*
Whose?	We ask who something belongs to.	*Whose is that car?*	*My father's.*
What?	We ask about things, actions or professions.	*What are you doing?* *What does your mum do?*	*I'm studying.* *She's a doctor.*
Which?	We ask about a person or a thing, when we have to choose from a limited number of people/things.	*Which of the three books is yours?*	*The big one.*
Where?	We ask about places.	*Where is dad?*	*In the garden.*
When?	We ask about time.	*When are you leaving?*	*Tomorrow.*
Why?	We ask about the reason why something happens.	*Why are you late?*	*Because I missed the bus.*
How?	We ask about the way in which something happens, or about someone's health.	*How do you go to school?* *How is your grandfather?*	*By bus.* *He's fine.*

Note: We use **how + adjective/adverb** when we ask for specific information.

How old are you?	*I'm twelve.*
How often do you visit her?	*Every weekend.*
How high is this building?	*About ninety metres.*
How far is the bank?	*It's only 300 metres from here.*
How long have you had this car?	*Since 1999.*

b Subject Questions – Object Questions

- **Subject Questions:** When we use the question words **who**, **which** and **what** to ask about the subject of the verb, we form the question without auxiliary verbs (**who/which/what + verb** in the **affirmative form**).

Who saw the accident?	*Tom (saw the accident).*
What happened outside?	*An accident (happened).*

- **Object Questions:** When we use the question words **who**, **which** and **what** to ask about the object of the verb, we form the question with auxiliary verbs (**who/which/what + verb** in the **interrogative form**).

Who did you see at the restaurant?	*(I saw) Tom and June.*
What are you eating?	*(I'm eating) Chinese food.*

activities

a **Complete the blanks with the question words in the box.**

who	when	whose	what	~~which~~	where	how	why

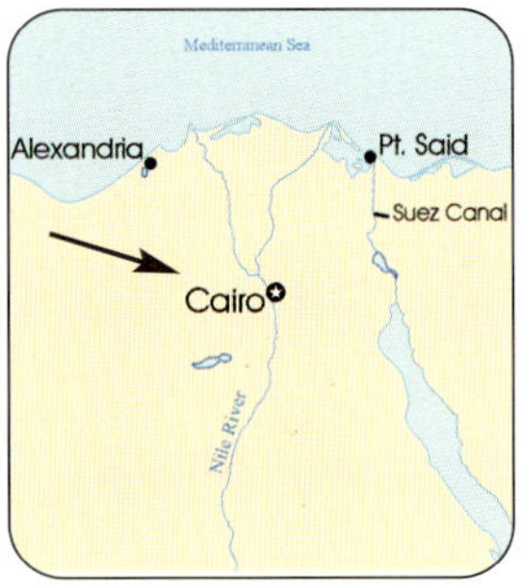

1 *Which* city is bigger, London or Cairo?
Cairo.

2 ____________ do kangaroos come from?
Australia.

3 ____________ discovered America?
Christopher Columbus.

4 ____________ colour is a polar bear?
White.

5 ____________ house is the White House?
The American President's.

6 ____________ many players are there in a volleyball team?
Six.

7 ____________ did man land on the moon for the first time?
In 1969.

8 ____________ do many people visit Egypt?
They want to see the Pyramids.

b **Circle the correct words.**

1 (**What**) / **Which** is your father's name?
2 **What** / **Which** country is the largest, Canada, China or Australia?
3 **What** / **Which** do elephants eat?
4 **Who** / **Which** of the two women is your teacher?
5 **What** / **Which** bag is yours, the red one or the brown one?
6 All three dresses are beautiful. **What** / **Which** one do you prefer?
7 **What** / **Which** time does the train for Salzburg leave?
8 **Who** / **Which** can speak German well?

c Complete the blanks in the dialogues with the words in the box.

long	far	tall	~~much~~	many	old

1 Andrew: How *much* money have you got?
Bob: I've got £15.
2 Kelly: How ____________ is your sister?
Joe: She's thirteen.
3 Mary: How ____________ is it from the bus stop to your school?
Tom: It's about two hundred metres.
4 Luke: How ____________ is your father?
Harry: 1.85.
5 Karen: How ____________ brothers and sisters have you got?
Brian: I've got one brother but I haven't got any sisters.
6 Carol: How ____________ have you had this car?
Debbie: For about six years.

d Look at the results of the football matches and answer the questions below.

Day 1			
ENGLAND	2	RUSSIA	1
JAPAN	0	ARGENTINA	3

Day 2			
RUSSIA	3	JAPAN	1
ENGLAND	2	ARGENTINA	2

Day 3			
JAPAN	0	ENGLAND	2
ARGENTINA	1	RUSSIA	2

1 Which team(s) did England beat?
Russia and Japan.

2 Which team(s) beat Japan?
____

3 Which team(s) beat Russia?
____

4 Which team(s) did Russia beat?
____

5 Which team(s) did Argentina beat?
____

6 Which team(s) beat Argentina?
____

e Write questions for the answers below. The words in bold type are the answers.

1 *What did Peter buy yesterday?*
Peter bought **a new camera** yesterday.

2 ____________________
Anna helped Kim clean the house after the party.

3 ____________________
Tina is wearing **the red** dress.

4 ____________________
Michael found **some money** in the street.

5 ______________________________

Paul saw **Lisa** in the cafeteria.

6 ______________________________

The vase fell on the floor.

f can you remember?

Circle the correct word(s).

1 **Who** / **How** will you get to school if you **will miss** / **miss** the bus?
2 **When** / **What** will we see the film if we **won't go** / **don't go** to the cinema tonight?
3 If all the people in your class come to the party, **what** / **how** many people **will be** / **are** there?
4 **What** / **How** will the children do if it **rains** / **will rain** this weekend?
5 If Thomas doesn't lend you his car, **whose** / **who** car **will you borrow** / **do you borrow**?
6 **Where** / **Why** will you go on holiday if you **will win** / **win** a lot of money?

g Communication

Work in pairs.

Student A Go to page 141

Student B Go to page 149

vocabulary box

address
mile
interest
foreign language
reason

h writing

Below is a letter from Julia to her new penfriend Christine. Julia wants to know a few things about Christine. Complete the paragraph with questions.

Now a few things about myself: I'm 13 years old. I've got two brothers and one sister. We all live on a farm, 15 miles from Cardiff, the nearest city. You see, my parents are both farmers. I study hard for school, especially maths, because I want to become a maths teacher. In my free time I read books, play computer games or watch films on TV or on the video. My favourite film star is Brad Pitt.

Can you tell me a few things about yourself? ....

....

....

....

Unit 18

Must
Have to
Should

Pet Problems

Two friends are chatting on the Internet. Read their conversation.

New Message

File Edit View Insert Format Tools Message Help

Robert says:
Hi Emily.

Emily says:
Hi Robert. How are you?

Robert says:
I'm fine. Can I ask you something?

Emily says:
Sure.

Robert says:
I **have to** come to the UK on business. Is it true that I **mustn't** bring my dog Fifi with me?

Emily says:
Well, it's not 100% true. In the past all dogs that arrived in the UK **had to** stay in a dogs' home for six months. Nowadays a dog **doesn't have to** go there if its owner has a certificate which says that the dog is healthy. Have you got a certificate?

Robert says:
No, and I haven't got the time to get one now. What **should** I do? **I have to** stay in the UK for a week.

Emily says:
Well, you **shouldn't** bring Fifi with you then. Anyway, you aren't staying very long. I think you **should** ask a friend to take care of her while you are away.

Robert says:
I guess you're right. Thanks Emily. See you soon.

Are the following sentences True or False? Write T or F in the boxes.

1 Robert wanted to take his dog to the UK. ☐
2 All dogs that arrive in the UK must stay in a dogs' home for six months. ☐
3 Robert can take his dog to the UK if he gets a certificate. ☐
4 Emily advises Robert to bring Fifi to the UK. ☐

Grammar

a Must

- **Must** is a **modal verb**. It is used only in the Present tense. It is the same in all persons, singular and plural. It forms the interrogative and negative without auxiliary verbs (do/does) and it is followed by a bare infinitive.
  I must go. *Must you leave?* *She mustn't stay.*

We use **must**:

- in the affirmative and interrogative to express **obligation**.
  I must study harder.
- in the negative **(mustn't)** to express **prohibition**.
  You mustn't walk on the grass.

b Have to

Affirmative	Negative
I have to go He/She/It has to go We/You/They have to go	I don't have to go He/She/It doesn't have to go We/You/They don't have to go

Interrogative	Short Answers	
Do I have to go? Does he/she/it have to go? Do we/you/they have to go?	Yes, I do. Yes, he/she/it does. Yes, we/you/they do.	No, I don't. No, he/she/it doesn't. No, we/you/they don't.

We use **have to**:

- In the affirmative and interrogative to express **obligation**.
  Students have to be at school by 8.30 am every day.
- In the negative to express **absence of obligation**, (= when something is not necessary). **Don't/doesn't have to** is not a synonym of **mustn't**.
  You don't have to come to work so early. *You mustn't be late for work.*

Notes:

- **Had to** expresses **obligation in the past**.
  Will have to expresses **obligation in the future**.
  She had to take six exams last year.
  She will have to take six exams next year.
- **Didn't have to** expresses **absence of obligation** in the **past**.
  Won't have to expresses **absence of obligation** in the **future**.
  Bruce had his camera with him, so I didn't have to take mine.
  Bruce will have his camera with him, so I won't have to take mine.

c Should

- **Should**, like **must**, is a **modal verb**.
  I should go. *Should they stay?* *She shouldn't leave.*

We use **should**:

- To give **advice**. *You should see a doctor.*
- To make a **suggestion**. *Maybe we should ask her about it.*
- To express an opinion. *I think he should tell his boss.*

activities

a **Look at the pictures and the prompts and write sentences. Use must / mustn't.**

1 wake up

He must wake up.

2 turn off / radio

____

3 park / there

____

4 shout / library

____

5 cross / street

____

6 wear / helmet

____

b **Complete the sentences with mustn't or don't have to.**

1 We *don't have to* go to school at the weekends.
2 You _______________ talk to the driver when you're on a bus.
3 You _______________ go to hospital, just take these pills.
4 We _______________ tell anybody, it's a secret.
5 You _______________ wear sunglasses if it's dark.
6 We _______________ sunbathe on the beach for too long.

c **Read the prompts below and write sentences. Use have to in the correct tense.**

1 Ben / drive / children / school / yesterday

Ben had to drive the children to school yesterday.

2 my parents / travel / Italy / next month

____

3 Lisa / not work / next year

____

4 Jim / not cook / dinner / last Sunday

____

5 the students / not finish / project / tomorrow

____

6 my sister / see / doctor / last week

____

d **Look at the pictures and the prompts and write questions and answers. Use have to.**

1 Mary / work / afternoon / ?
→ No / morning

Does Mary have to work in the afternoon?
No, she doesn't. She has to work in the morning.

2 John / buy / ticket / ?
→ No

____

3 your brothers / clean / room / every day / ?
→ No / weekend

____

4 babies / drink / milk / ?
→ Yes

____

5 Carol / study / history / tonight / ?
→ No / geography

____

6 they / wear / uniform / ?
→ Yes

____

e **Look at the prompts and write sentences. Use should or shouldn't.**

1 Ben has got a toothache.
eat / sweets — *He shouldn't eat sweets.*
go / dentist's — *He should go to the dentist's.*

2 Kevin isn't good at maths.
pay attention / in class ______________
study harder ______________

3 John has hurt his leg.
not walk ______________
stay / bed ______________

4 Diane wants to relax.
listen / music ______________
have / bath ______________

5 Dennis is late for work.
wait / bus ______________
take / taxi ______________

6 Lisa has got a cold.
go / out ______________
eat / ice-cream ______________

f can you remember?

Write questions for the answers below. Ask about the words in bold type.

1 *How many books did you have to return to the library?*

I had to return **two** books to the library.

2 ______________________________

Martha should take the dog for a walk.

3 ______________________________

The baby must eat **some soup** for dinner.

4 ______________________________

You should buy **the green** dress for your mother.

5 ______________________________

My sister has to call her boss **this afternoon**.

6 ______________________________

The teacher should read **Kelly's** story to the class.

g Communication

Work in pairs. Read Tara's and Peggy's problems below and discuss what each of them should/shouldn't do. Use ideas from the vocabulary box.

I want to lose weight but I don't know what to do.

I've been working hard and I feel very tired and stressed. What should I do?

vocabulary box

go on a diet
see a doctor
exercise
sleep more
drink soft drinks
eat sweets
go on holiday
worry too much

e.g. **A :** *I think Tara/Peggy should/shouldn't...*
B : *I also think she should/shouldn't...*

h writing

Write a few sentences about:

two things you have to do at home ....

....

two things you mustn't do at home ....

....

two things you don't have to do at home ....

....

Revision Units 15-18

a Read the sentences below. Write sentences using the Future *Will* and the prompts in the box.

pass/exams   be/London/two hours   ~~cook/spaghetti/dinner~~   buy/orange juice and coke   be/late

1 
I haven't eaten spaghetti for a long time. *I'll cook spaghetti for dinner.*

2 
Mary hasn't bought any drinks for the party yet. ______________________ ______________________

3 
Wendy is a good student and always studies hard. ______________________ ______________________

4  
Let's meet outside the cinema at half past six. And don't worry. ______________________ ______________________

5 
Danny left Bristol half an hour ago. ______________________ ______________________ ______________________

b Complete the blanks with the Future *Going to* of the verbs in brackets.

1 The Tigers are playing better than the Lions. They *are going to win* (win) the game.

2 Linda: What ______________________ (you / do) tonight?
Stephanie: I ______________________ (stay) at home and watch TV.

3 Betty has hurt her finger and she ______________________ (not play) the guitar today.

4 Jenny: ______________________ (Steve / call) Diane?
Brian: No, he ______________________ (send) her an e-mail.

5 Albert: Where ______________________ (you/spend) your summer holidays?
Kelly: My sister and I ______________________ (travel) around Europe.

c Complete the blanks with the Present Simple or the Future *Will* of the verbs in brackets.

1 I *will have* (have) lunch when I *get* (get) hungry.
2 After Sue and Bill ______________ (get married), they ______________ (build) a house.
3 Peter ______________ (not do) anything until he ______________ (tell) his parents.
4 John ______________ (visit) us before he ______________ (fly) to the USA.
5 When I ______________ (finish) work this afternoon, I ______________ (go) to the beach.
6 ______________ (you / feed) the cat before you ______________ (leave) tomorrow?

d **Look at the pictures, read the sentences and answer the questions. Use Conditional Sentences Type 1, as in the example.**

1 It might rain tomorrow. What will Peter do?

If it rains tomorrow, Peter will play computer games.

If it doesn't rain tomorrow, Peter will go swimming.

2 Fiona's friends might visit her tomorrow. What will she do?

____

____

3 Charlie and George may go camping tomorrow. What will they do?

____

____

4 Tina may finish work early this afternoon. What will she do?

____

____

e **Write questions for the answers below. Ask about the words in bold type.**

1 *Where does Alicia live?*

Alicia lives **in Warsaw**, **Poland**.

2 ______________________________

Alex met **Kevin** yesterday.

3 ______________________________

Harriet's dog is playing in the garden.

4 ______________________________

Meg bought **apples and oranges** at the greengrocer's.

5 ______________________________

The teacher asked Phil a question.

6 ______________________________

Tina is unhappy **because she lost her watch**.

7 ______________________________

Linda usually goes to school **by bus**.

8 ______________________________

Tony's leaving **next Saturday**.

f Complete the blanks with mustn't or don't / doesn't have to.

1 Kelly is very clever. She *doesn't have to* study hard for her exams.

2 The baby is sleeping. You ______________ make any noise.

3 You ______________ come to the party if you're tired.

4 People ______________ cross the street when the light is red.

5 Kate can borrow her sister's car for the holidays. She ______________ hire one.

6 You ______________ lie to your mother. It's not right.

g Look at the pictures and the prompts and write sentences. Use should or shouldn't.

exercise

1 Amy *shouldn't exercise.*

have / shower

2 Keith ______________

do / washing-up

3 Bart ______________

go / near / tiger

4 Bob ______________

tidy

5 Tanya ______________

carry

6 Mrs Green ______________

h Choose *a*, *b* or *c*.

1 I'll wait *until* you finish shopping.
a. until (circled) **b.** after **c.** before

2 Pay attention or I ______________ you again!
a. am not helping **b.** don't help **c.** won't help

3 You ______________ go to the doctor if your ears hurt.
a. may **b.** must **c.** have

4 ______________ fast can Julie run?
a. What **b.** Which **c.** How

5 In the past many children couldn't go to school because they ______________ work.
a. have to **b.** didn't have to **c.** had to

6 ______________ George drives carefully, he may have an accident.
a. Unless **b.** If **c.** When

7 ______________ lamp did you put in your room, the old one or the new one?
a. What **b.** Which **c.** Whose

8 I ______________ work harder next year.
a. will have to **b.** will must **c.** had to

Unit 19

Negative Questions
Question Tags

You're an actress, aren't you?

Complete the dialogue below with the sentences a-e.

a Yes, I am.

b I do.

c No, that was Angelina Jolie.

d Well, no. He's Catherine Zeta Jones' husband.

e Yes, it's not bad.

Man: It's a great party, **isn't it**?
Woman: (**1**) _______
Man: Hey! I know you. **Aren't you** an actress?
Woman: (**2**) _______
Man: I can't remember your name, but you **played** Lara Croft in the film *Tomb Raider*, **didn't you**?
Woman: (**3**) _______
Man: Oh, yes of course... Sorry... You don't come from the USA, **do you**?
Woman: (**4**) _______
Man: Sorry again. Just a minute. I remember you now. Michael Douglas is your husband, **isn't he**?
Woman: (**5**) _______
Man: Mm, yes... Anyway, let's dance, **shall we**?

Grammar

a Negative Questions

Negative questions are formed with the **auxiliary verb + not** in the short form + **subject** (Aren't you...?, Didn't Mary...?, Haven't the children...?, etc.).

We use **negative questions**:

- To show **surprise**.
  Haven't you done your homework yet? It's half past ten!
- When we expect the person we are speaking to to **agree** with us.
  Isn't your husband an electrician? Yes, he is.

b Question Tags

Question tags are short questions which are placed at the end of statements.

- Question tags are formed with the **auxiliary or modal verb** of the sentence and a **personal pronoun** in the same person as the subject. If the sentence does not contain an auxiliary or a modal verb, we use **do**, **does** or **did**, depending on the tense of the verb.
  John is a doctor, isn't he?
  Peter and Marion passed the test, didn't they?
  You can swim, can't you?
- Question tags take **not** when the sentence is **affirmative**.
  You have visited Egypt, haven't you?
- Question tags **don't** take **not** when the sentence is **negative**.
  You haven't visited Egypt, have you?

We use **question tags:**

- When we **are not sure** about something and we want to confirm it. In this case, the tone of the voice goes up.
  Mr Thompson is an English teacher, isn't he? Yes, he is. / No, he isn't.
- When we **are sure** about something and we expect the person we are speaking to to agree with what we are saying. In this case, the tone of the voice goes down.
  Mr Thompson is a very good teacher, isn't he? Of course he is.

Notes:

- Pay attention to the following question tags:
  I'm a good cook, aren't I?
  Let's go out, shall we?
  There's somebody at the door, isn't there?
- We use a comma to separate the question tag from the main sentence.

activities

a Read the situations below and write negative questions.

1 You are surprised because your friend can't ride a bicycle.

Can't you ride a bicycle?

2 You see somebody on the bus and you think that you have met before. What do you say to him/her?

____

3 You believe that your friend's sister speaks French. What do you say to your friend?

____

4 You are at a restaurant with your family and you think that the pizza is awful. What do you say?

____

5 You are surprised because your brother isn't studying for his maths test. What do you say to him?

____

6 You go to your friend's party but the other guests haven't arrived yet. What do you say?

____

b Match the sentences with the question tags.

1 Jenny's parents aren't very old, → c
2 The boys have already seen that film,
3 Kelly's brothers are your best friends,
4 Henry went to London last year,
5 The plans haven't changed,
6 Their father doesn't smoke,
7 George always helps his friends,
8 Roger didn't buy you a present,

a didn't he?
b aren't they?
c are they?
d have they?
e does he?
f haven't they?
g did he?
h doesn't he?

c Circle the correct question tag.

1 The weather is wonderful, (**isn't it**) / **is it** ?
2 Mark was at Mary's birthday party on Saturday, **was he** / **wasn't he** ?
3 Helen can't play the guitar, **can she** / **can Helen**?
4 You haven't seen my sunglasses anywhere, **did you** / **have you** ?

5 David bought a new bicycle yesterday, **wasn't he** / **didn't he** ?

6 Karen isn't doing her homework, **is she** / **does she** ?

d Complete the blanks in the sentences with question tags.

1 I didn't scare you, ___*did I*___ ?

2 Linda likes skiing, ______________ ?

3 Jim's mother couldn't find him anywhere, ______________ ?

4 Mr Miller hasn't found a job yet, ______________ ?

5 You and Kate went out last night, ______________ ?

6 Carl and his wife earn a lot of money, ______________ ?

7 I'm right, ______________ ?

8 Your parents will help you, ______________ ?

e Complete the blanks in the dialogues with question tags.

1 **Debbie:** Good morning Miss. I'm not late, (**1**) ___*am I*___ ?

Teacher: No, you're not. Sit down, please. OK class, let's check your homework now, (**2**) __________ ?

Emily: Miss, we didn't have any homework for today, (**3**) __________ ?

Teacher: Oh, you're right, I didn't give you any homework yesterday, (**4**) __________? Well then, I should give you an exercise to do now, (**5**) __________ ?

John: Miss, it won't be very difficult, (**6**) __________ ?

2 **Anna:** Mrs Peterson, there is a game on Friday, (**7**) __________ ? Who will play on the team?

Mrs Peterson: Yes, there is a game and Tina, Emma, Kim, Helga and Juanita will play.

Anna: Why can't I play? I'm a good player, (**8**) __________ ?

Mrs Peterson: Yes, but you don't train very often. You haven't trained for a week now, (**9**) __________ ?

Anna: Well, no, I haven't, but...

Mrs Peterson: I'm sorry, Anna, but unless you train every day, you can't play on the team. That is the rule. We can't change it just for you, (**10**) __________ ?

f Read the situations below and write sentences with question tags.

1 You think that your friend's dog is very clever. What do you say to your friend?

Your dog is very clever, isn't it?

2 You think that Ricky Martin sings very well. What do you say to your friend?

____

3 You went to a concert with your friend last night and you think it was fantastic. What do you say to your friend?

____

4 You and your friend want to make a cake but you believe that there aren't enough eggs. What do you say to your friend?

____

5 You are not sure if your dad has fed the dog. What do you say to your mum?

____

6 You believe that the students at your friend's school recycle paper but you are not sure. What do you say to your friend?

____

7 You want to go to the theatre with your friend. What do you say to your friend?

____

g can you remember?

Circle the correct words and complete the blanks with question tags.

1 We **have** / **must** to paint the house, ___*don't we*___ ?

2 We **should** / **shouldn't** protect the environment, ________________ ?

3 Kate **must** / **had to** work at the weekends last year, ________________ ?

4 People **mustn't** / **don't have to** walk on the grass in the park, ________________ ?

5 If they want to win the game, they will **have to** / **must** play very well, ________________ ?

6 I **mustn't** / **don't have to** brush my teeth six times a day, ________________ ?

h Communication

Work in pairs.

Student A Go to page 141

Student B Go to page 149

vocabulary box

actor	star in
director	direct
athlete	win/medal
runner	do the long jump

i writing

Write five sentences which finish with the question tags given.

1 ...., didn't he?

2 ...., are they?

3 ...., doesn't she?

4 ...., is there?

5 ...., shall we?

Unit 20

Passive Voice

Magazine articles

Read the texts below.

booksbooksbooksbooksbooksbooksbooksbooksbooks

Netronic is a science fiction book which will certainly become a bestseller. The book is about a city which **is controlled** by machines. *Netronic* **was written** by John Bates two years ago and it **will be published** by T. S. Dwight next month.

What's the difference between *Peking duck* and *Bombay duck*?

Peking duck is a Chinese dish. It **is made** from duck and it got its name from the capital city of China, which **is** now **called** Beijing. *Bombay duck* **is eaten** in India and it **has been named** after the Indian city Bombay. However, it **is not made** from duck, but from a fish which **is called** bummalo. Nobody knows why this dish **is called** *Bombay duck*.

Now answer the following questions.

1 Who wrote *Netronic*?

a. John Bates **b.** T. S. Dwight

2 Can you read *Netronic* now?

a. Yes, it came out two years ago. **b.** No, it will come out next month.

3 What do you eat when you eat *Bombay duck*?

a. duck **b.** fish

4 Where do people eat *Bombay duck*?

a. In India. **b.** In China.

Grammar

Passive Voice

The **Active Voice** shows that the subject of the verb does an action.

Mary washes the clothes once a week.

Passive Voice

- The **Passive Voice** shows that something happens to the subject of the verb.
  The clothes are washed by Mary once a week.
- It is used when we want to emphasise the action rather than the person who does it.

Note:
- The person or thing that causes or carries out the action is called an **agent** and is introduced by the preposition **by**. We omit **by + agent** when we don't know or when it is easy to understand who the agent is.
  The building has been sold. *English is spoken in Australia (by people).*

- We form the **Passive Voice** with the verb **be** in the appropriate tense and the **past participle** of the main verb.

Tense	Formation	Example
Present Simple	I am He/She/It is washed We/You/They are	*The clothes are washed every week.*
Past Simple	I/He/She/It was We/You/They were washed	*The clothes were washed yesterday.*
Future *Will*	I/He/She/It We/You/They will be washed	*The clothes will be washed tomorrow.*
Present Perfect	He/She/It has been I/We/You/They have been washed	*The clothes have been washed.*

- We form the interrogative and negative sentences in **Passive Voice** with the interrogative and negative form of the verb **be**.

Are the clothes washed every day?
Was the letter written yesterday?
The presents have not / haven't been bought yet.
The clothes will not / won't be washed tomorrow.

Transformation from Active to Passive Voice

Transforming a sentence from the **Active Voice** to the **Passive Voice**:

- The **object** of the verb in the **Active Voice** becomes the **subject** in the **Passive Voice**.
- We put the verb **be** in the same tense as the verb in the **Active Voice**.
- We put the main verb into the **past participle**.
- If we want to show who does the action (**agent**), we use the preposition **by** with the subject of the active verb.

	Subject	Verb	Object
Active Voice	Mary	wrote	a letter.
	Subject	**Verb**	**Agent**
Passive Voice	A letter	was written	by Mary.

activities

a Complete the blanks with the Present Simple Passive of the verbs in brackets.

1 English ___*is spoken*___ (speak) all over the world.
2 Paper ______________ (recycle) by many people.
3 Water sports ______________ (enjoy) by lots of people.
4 Maths ______________ (teach) at most schools.
5 Many animals ______________ (kill) every year.
6 Some fish ______________ (not catch) easily.
7 ______________ (computers/use) in your school?
8 My friend ______________ (not call) Sophie. Her name is Joanne.

b Complete the blanks with the Past Simple Passive of the verbs in the box.

~~sell~~	invent	take	not feed	build	steal	plant

1 The old boat ___*was sold*___ last year.
2 This picture ______________ in Switzerland.
3 Tom's car ______________ last week. He hasn't found it yet.
4 Those flowers ______________ by my mother.
5 When ______________ the telephone ______________ ?
6 This bridge ______________ in 1890.
7 The goldfish ______________ yesterday. Give it some food.

c Complete the blanks with the Present Perfect Passive of the verbs in brackets.

1 **Kelly:** Is there any cake in the fridge?
Mum: No, there isn't. All the cake ___*has been eaten*___ (eat).

2 **Customer:** Have you got any green jackets?
Shop assistant: No, I'm sorry, all the green jackets ______________ (sell).

3 **Dennis:** Is everything ready for the party?
Patty: Well, the food ______________ (prepare) and the room ______________ (decorate), but the music ______________ (not choose) yet.

4 Eddie: ____________________ (your dog/find) yet?
Emma: No, we're still looking for it.

5 Claire: Why is Michael afraid of bees?
Fay: Well, maybe because he ____________________ (sting) by bees twice.

d Circle the Active or the Passive Voice.

1. Tina's parents (**have lived**) / **have been lived** in that house for twenty-five years.
2. A lot of money **will spend** / **will be spent** on space travel in the future.
3. Diane **asked** / **was asked** her brother to help her.
4. Will petrol **use** / **be used** in a hundred years from now?
5. When **did this book write** / **was this book written**?
6. Kate **has collected** / **has been collected** lots of stamps from different countries.
7. This jacket **made** / **was made** in the USA.
8. Lisa **drives** / **is driven** her children to school every day.
9. Jeans are very popular. They **wear** / **are worn** all over the world.
10. The tickets **won't buy** / **won't be bought** until Monday.

e Use the prompts to write sentences. Use the Present Simple Passive of the verbs.

1. hundreds / letters / send / every day
   Hundreds of letters are sent every day.
2. rice / grow / water
   ____
3. milk / keep / fridge
   ____
4. homework / do / always / home
   ____
5. our house / paint / every five years
   ____
6. this museum /visited /two million people /every year
   ____

f can you remember?

Add question tags to the sentences and write answers in the Passive Voice.

1. Percy's dog bit Carol yesterday, *didn't it* ?
   Yes, *Carol was bitten by Percy's dog yesterday.*
2. They will fix the computer soon, ____________ ?
   Yes, ____________________

3 People speak English in Australia, ______________ ?

Yes, ____

4 Mother has already cooked dinner, ______________ ?

Yes, ____

5 Your brother hid that book, ______________ ?

Yes, ____

6 They will build a swimming pool on Rose Street, ______________ ?

Yes, ____

g Communication

Work in pairs.

Student A Go to page 142

Student B Go to page 150

vocabulary box

invent
discover
direct

h writing

Look at the pictures and write a paragraph. Use the prompts given and the Past Simple Passive.

- police car / park / outside / bank / when / it / hit / bus
- police car / damage

- luckily / no-one / kill / but / two women / injure
- ambulance / call / immediately / and / women / take / hospital

- bus driver / take / police station

An accident took place yesterday afternoon at the corner of Hill Street and Wellington Road.

Unit 21

Past Perfect Simple

Had she been careful?

Read the text below.

A careful driver?

They say that women drive more carefully than men. Mrs Choo thought she was a careful driver, but is that true? Read on and find out.

One evening after she **had done** her shopping, she went to the car park, got into her car and drove to the exit. There was a lot of traffic on the main road, so she had to wait. She waited patiently for five hours! By the time the traffic got less, Mrs Choo **had fallen** asleep because she was too tired. When she woke up the next morning, the traffic **had increased** again. Mrs Choo waited for another two hours, and then she decided it was time to go home. However, as she drove quickly out onto the main road, she heard a big bang. In her rush she **had hit** a police car!

So, what do you think? Had Mrs Choo been careful?

Which of the two actions happened first, a or b? Tick (✓) the correct boxes.

1 **a.** Mrs Choo drove to the exit of the car park. ☐
b. Mrs Choo did her shopping. ☐

2 **a.** The traffic became less. ☐
b. Mrs Choo fell asleep in the car. ☐

3 **a.** Mrs Choo woke up. ☐
b. The traffic increased. ☐

Grammar

Past Perfect Simple

We use the **Past Perfect Simple**:

- For an action which took place before a specific point of time in the past.
  She had finished her homework before 8 o'clock.
- For an action which took place before another one in the past (in time clauses with **before**, **after**, **when**, **by the time**). We use the **Past Perfect Simple** for the first action and the **Past Simple** for the action that followed.
  I watched TV after I had finished my homework.
  The train had gone by the time we arrived at the station.

Time Expressions
before + point in time
by + point in time

Time Expressions
before, after, when
by the time

We form the **Past Perfect Simple** with **had** and the **Past Participle** of the verb.

Affirmative		Negative	
FULL FORMS	SHORT FORMS	FULL FORMS	SHORT FORMS
I had written	I'd written	I had not written	I hadn't written
He/She/It had written	He/She/It'd written	He/She/It had not written	He/She/It hadn't written
We/You/They had written	We/You/They'd written	We/You/They had not written	We/You/They hadn't written

Interrogative	Short Answers	
Had I written?	Yes, I had.	No, I hadn't.
Had he/she/it written?	Yes, he/she/it had.	No, he/she/it hadn't.
Had we/you/they written?	Yes, we/you/they had.	No, we/you/they hadn't.

Note: The Past Perfect Simple of the verb **have** is **had had**.
I had had dinner when they called me.

activities

a **Look at the pictures and the prompts and write questions and answers. Use the Past Perfect Simple.**

1 Erica / call / her friends / before she visited them?
Had Erica called her friends before she visited them?
Yes, she had.

2 Lee / take off / shoes / before he entered the room?
____

3 Nadia / finish / work / by 7:00?
____

4 Mandy and her children / brush / teeth / before they went to bed?

____
____
____
____

5 Helen / be / hairdresser's / before she went to the party?

____
____
____
____

6 the train / leave / when Mrs Lewis arrived at the station?

____
____
____
____

b Complete the blanks in the sentences with the Past Perfect Simple of the verbs in brackets.

1 Mrs Asher *had made* (make) sandwiches before the children returned from school.
2 The students asked questions after the teacher __________ (explain) the exercise.
3 Donna __________ (feed) the baby by eight o'clock.
4 By the time Jenny gave her test to the teacher, she __________ (check) it twice.
5 When Ron brought the soft drinks, his friends __________ (cut) the cake.

c Complete the blanks with the Past Simple or the Past Perfect Simple of the verbs in brackets.

1 Fiona *had learnt* (learn) Italian before she *went* (go) to Rome.
2 Emma __________ (watch) TV after she __________ (do) her homework.
3 By the time Jerry and Emily __________ (get) to the cinema, the film __________ (start).
4 I __________ (not finish) my project when Vivian __________ (call) me.
5 After we __________ (eat) dinner, we __________ (go) out for a walk.
6 Kelly __________ (not have) breakfast before she __________ (leave) for school.

d Join the sentences. Use the time expressions given and the Past Perfect Simple.

1 Kim read the book. Then she saw the film. **before**

Kim had read the book before she saw the film.

2 Linda cut the vegetables into small pieces. Then she cooked them. **after**

____

3 Luke made the coffee. Then Wendy woke up. **by the time**

____

4 Emily bought a computer. Then she learnt how to use it. — before

____

5 The bank robber ran away. Then the police arrived. — when

____

6 The guests left. Then, Ken arrived home. — by the time

____

e can you remember?

Circle the correct word(s).

1. David (opened) / **was opening** the door and **let** / **was letting** the dog in.
2. Henry **lived** / **has lived** in London since 1997, but he **didn't visit** / **hasn't visited** Madame Tussaud's Museum yet.
3. By ten o'clock Wendy **packed** / **had packed** her suitcase and she **was** / **has been** ready to go.
4. Julie **slept** / **was sleeping** while George **studied** / **was studying**.
5. Ronnie **has never played** / **never played** badminton, but last year he **has tried** / **tried** bungee-jumping.
6. Sandy **wrote** / **was writing** a letter when Mark **called** / **was calling** her.
7. By the time my friends **arrived** / **had arrived**, I **cooked** / **had cooked** dinner.

f Communication

Work in pairs.

Student A Go to page 143

Student B Go to page 151

vocabulary box

form band	spend/make money
get/leave job	star in film
make record	win award
become famous	

g writing

Look at the newspaper headline below. Yesterday, a rescue team saved a young boy in the mountains of Tibet. What had happened before they found him? Use the prompts to write sentences.

PLANE CRASH IN TIBET
Young boy saved

- plane / crash / mountain
- everyone else / die
- boy / break / leg / and / hurt / back
- boy / find / cave / and / hide / there

....
....
....
....
....
....
....

Unit 22

So / Neither
Both / All
Neither / None

Both of them or neither of them?

Look at the picture and read the speech bubbles.

Answer the following questions by writing the correct letter. In some questions more than one letter can be correct.

Which of the people above

1 likes the dresses? ______________

2 doesn't like the dresses? ______________

3 must go on a diet? ______________

4 has difficulty finding a hat? ______________

Grammar

a So / Neither

We use **so + auxiliary verb + subject**:

- When we want to **agree** with an **affirmative statement**.
  I am a student. So am I.
  Paul likes chocolate. So does Helen.

We use **neither + auxiliary verb + subject**:

- When we want to **agree** with a **negative statement**.
  She's not a teacher. Neither is he.
  I haven't been to Portugal. Neither have I.

b Both / All / Neither / None

We use **both**:

- To show that something is true for **two** people or things.

  Jenny and Louise are friends. *They both go to school.*
  Both of them are good students.

We use **all**:

- To show that something is true for **more than two** people or things.

  Nick, Laura and Tom live in London. *They are all students.*
  All of them study Mathematics.

Notes:

- **Both** and **all** are used in affirmative sentences and always take a **plural** verb.
- **Both** and **all** are used alone or are followed by **subject** or **of + noun/pronoun.** When they refer to the subject of the sentence, they can be placed at the beginning of the sentence or before the main verb but after the verb *be*.
  All/Both (of) my sons can speak English.
  All/Both of them can speak English.
  My sons can all/both speak English.
  They can all/both speak English.

We use **neither**:

- To show that something is not true for **either of two** people or things.
  Jenny and Louise are friends. *Neither of them likes football.*

We use **none**:

- To show that something is not true for **more than two** people or things.
  Nick, Laura and Tom live in London. *None of them likes the city.*

Notes:
- **Neither** and **none** are used in affirmative sentences, but with a negative meaning.
- **Neither** and **none** are usually followed by **of + noun/pronoun**. The verb can be in the **singular or plural** form.

  Neither of us is/are English.
  None of these people speak/speaks English.

activities

a Match the sentences 1-10 with the responses a-j.

1 Alicia can't swim.
2 John doesn't walk to school.
3 Ben didn't eat lunch.
4 I haven't done my homework.
5 Emma and Cathy will go swimming tomorrow.
6 Kelly has finished her project.
7 I can speak Italian.
8 John passed the test.
9 My grandparents live in Oxford.
10 I won't go to Kate's party.

a So will Mary.
b So has Tom.
c Neither has Bruce.
d So do mine.
e Neither do I.
f So can my brother.
g Neither can Patricia.
h Neither did Simon.
i Neither will Tim.
j So did Stephen.

b Complete the sentences with so or neither + auxiliary verb.

1 Tom isn't on the football team and ___*neither is*___ George.
2 I like chocolate ice-cream and ________________ my sister.
3 Marcia won't go camping next year and ________________ Karen.
4 Carol hasn't bought a computer and ________________ Harry.
5 My friends watched a film on TV last night and ________________ I.
6 Michelle can speak English very well and ________________ Louise.
7 Mary is doing her homework and ________________ John.
8 Penny and Tina don't want to drink coffee and ________________ Sonia.

c Look at the pictures and complete the blanks with all, both, none or neither.

1 ___*None*___ of my friends wear glasses.

2 ____________ of the girls have got black hair.

3 ____________ of the women have got children.

4 ___________ of the boys have bought anything.

5 ___________ of the girls are laughing.

6 ___________ of the men are playing the guitar.

7 ___________ of the women are running.

8 ___________ of the people want to buy a ticket.

9 ___________ of the musicians are singing.

d **Look at the pictures and the prompts and write sentences. Use all, both, none, neither + of them.**

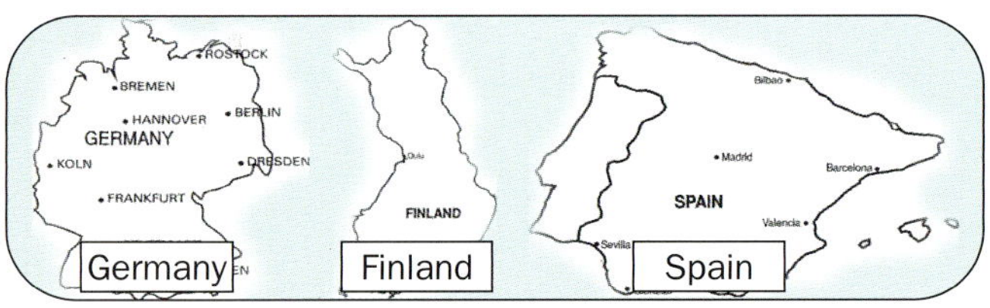

1 Europe : *All of them are in Europe.*
Asia: *None of them is/are in Asia.*

2 eat meat : ______________________
eat grass: ______________________

3 vegetables: ______________________
fruit: ______________________

4 live Africa : ______________________
live Europe: ______________________

5 London: ____________________

New York: ____________________

6 flowers: ____________________

trees: ____________________

e Rewrite the sentences using the words in brackets and both or all.

1 Dennis is tall and Sam is tall, too.
(boys) *Both boys are tall.*
(they) *They are both tall.*

2 Sarah plays the guitar and Helen plays the guitar, too.
(girls) ____________________
____
(they) ____________________

3 Everyone from Crestville High went to the zoo.
(students) ____________________
____
(they) ____________________

4 The cheetah can run fast and so can the zebra.
(animals) ____________________
____
(they) ____________________

5 Everybody enjoyed themselves at the party.
(people) ____________________
____
(they) ____________________

6 Vienna is beautiful and so is Paris.
(cities) ____________________
____
(they) ____________________

f can you remember?

Read the sentences below. Circle the correct words and put the verbs in brackets into the Present Simple Passive or the Past Simple Passive.

1 Ted has got three cars and **both** / **all** of them *were made* (make) in Japan.

2 There were four people in the car that crashed into the wall. Fortunately, **none** / **neither** of them ____________________ (kill).

3 Those two houses are very old. **Both** / **All** of them ____________________ (build) in the 17th century.

4 Souvenirs ____________________ (sell) in **all** / **none** the shops in the main square.

5 **Both** / **Neither** of these letters ____________________ (write) by Angela. This is not her handwriting.

6 Mr Wilson and his wife had an accident and **both** / **all** of them ____________________ (take) to hospital.

7 **Neither** / **None** of these boys ____________________ (call) Simon. Their names are Paul and Jack.

g Communication

Work in pairs.
Discuss with your partner to find things that both of you have done and things that neither of you have done. Use the ideas in the vocabulary box, your own ideas and *so/neither*, as in the example. Then, report to the rest of the class using *both* and *neither*.

vocabulary box

bungee-jumping
ice-skating
hang-gliding
explore caves

e.g. **A:** *I have tried bungee-jumping.*
B: *So have I.*
B: *I have never been ice-skating.*
A: *Neither have I.*

h writing

Imagine that you went on holiday with a friend last summer. Write a few sentences about what you both did and what neither of you did.

....

....

....

....

....

....

....

....

....

....

Revision Units 19-22

a Complete the sentences with question tags.

1 That isn't Billy's parrot, *is it* ?
2 She has travelled to Morocco, ____________ ?
3 I'm taller than Ben, ____________ ?
4 Nelly won't come to the party, ____________ ?
5 Let's make some popcorn, ____________ ?
6 You like milk, ____________ ?
7 Your friends didn't find the restaurant, ____________ ?
8 Peter isn't working today, ____________ ?
9 Your parents weren't at the school concert last week, ____________ ?
10 Ann doesn't like skating, ____________ ?
11 You haven't invited Mary to the party, ____________ ?
12 Steve was studying yesterday evening, ____________ ?

b Circle the correct words.

1 People in Canada **speak** / **are spoken** English and French.
2 A new concert hall **has built** / **has been built** in the city.
3 The planet Pluto **discovered** / **was discovered** in 1930.
4 Ann **will spend** / **will be spent** a lot of money on her sister's present.
5 Cars **are made** / **make** in this factory.
6 People **have hunted** / **have been hunted** animals for centuries.
7 Robots **will use** / **will be used** more in the future.
8 The woman **helped** / **was helped** her daughter buy a dress.

c Use the prompts below to write sentences. Use the Present Simple Passive, the Past Simple Passive, the Present Perfect Passive and the Future Passive.

1 Jack / beat / chess / his sister / yesterday

Jack was beaten at chess by his sister yesterday.

2 windows / clean / every week

____

3 presents / already / buy

____

4 new library / finish / in 2009

____

5 fifty cameras / steal / last night

____

6 Christmas / celebrate / millions / people / every year

____

7 letter / send / tomorrow

____

8 these shoes / make / Italy

____

d **Complete the sentences with the Past Simple or the Past Perfect Simple of the verbs in brackets.**

1 Jenny ____*had left*____ (leave) the house when her son ______________ (burn) his hand.
2 John ______________ (be) very hungry yesterday evening because he ______________ (not eat) anything all day.
3 By the time my parents ______________ (decide) to go for a walk, the weather ______________ (change).
4 When Melissa ______________ (arrive) at her office, she ______________ (remember) that she ______________ (not lock) the door of her house.
5 Dennis ______________ (do) his homework before he ______________ (watch) TV.
6 Donald ______________ (prepare) the salad after he ______________ (cook) dinner.

e **Complete the blanks with so or neither + auxiliary verb.**

1 My mother is a nurse. ____*So is*____ mine.
2 Helen never wears a dress. ______________ Tina.
3 We won't go camping this summer. ______________ we.
4 Ben and Ted joined the water-polo team. ______________ John.
5 Carla has already left the party. ______________ Gina and Emily.
6 I haven't seen John at school this week. ______________ I.
7 My brothers enjoy skiing very much. ______________ my friends.
8 George and Fred were very noisy when they were young. ______________ their sister.
9 Phoebe didn't travel to Brazil last year. ______________ John.
10 Kim isn't cleaning her room now. ______________ I.

f Rewrite the sentences starting with both, all, neither or none + of.

1 Ben, Nick and Keith are my brothers. They don't work.

None of my brothers works/work.

2 Elaine and Penelope are my best friends. They live very far from my house.

____

3 Tony, Sarah and Erica are teachers. They were very busy last week.

____

4 Mr and Mrs Miller are my parents. They never eat spaghetti.

____

5 Diane, Kelly and Tom are my classmates. They aren't having a lesson now.

____

6 Mark and Perry are students. They passed the exam.

____

7 Mrs Davies and Mrs Green are our neighbours. They haven't got a pet.

____

8 Eddie, Fred and Greg are football players. They run very fast.

____

g Choose *a*, *b* or *c*.

1 Most people like chocolate, *don't they* ?
a. aren't they **b.** doesn't it **c.** don't they

2 Kelly and Tom had a lot of homework last weekend. ________ of them could go out.
a. Neither **b.** Both **c.** None

3 Ann's wallet ________ . It's at the police station.
a. found **b.** is found **c.** has been found

4 There were many people around but ________ of them saw the accident.
a. none **b.** all **c.** neither

5 Tina's dress ________ very carefully for the party.
a. had ironed **b.** has ironed **c.** was ironed

6 By the time they arrived at the beach, it ________ raining.
a. had started **b.** started **c.** has been started

7 Tina's dog ________ Prince, not Rex!
a. has called **b.** is called **c.** called

8 Betty and her family were living in London last year, ________ ?
a. were they **b.** weren't they **c.** wasn't it

9 The sweets ________ after everyone finishes dinner.
a. will be served **b.** will serve **c.** will served

10 The students in Mrs Stevenson's class are ________ very clever.
a. all **b.** both **c.** none

11 Emily hasn't worn those trousers before, ________ ?
a. does she **b.** have they **c.** has she

Pairwork activities
STUDENT A

Unit 1

The chart below shows what the Brown family usually do on Saturday morning and what they're doing today. Your partner has got the same chart, but different information is missing. Ask him/her questions to complete your chart. Use the ideas in the vocabulary box. Then, answer your partner's questions.

vocabulary box

watch cartoons
clean room
wash car
have coffee with friend
skate with friends
go on picnic
go shopping
work in garden

	Mrs Brown	Mr Brown	Tom	Betty and Judy
usually		?		?
today	?		?	

e.g. **A:** *Is Mrs Brown working in the garden today?*
B: *Yes, she is. / No, she isn't. She's...*

Pairwork activities

STUDENT A

Unit 4

Who lives where? Look at the picture below and ask your partner questions to match the people with their houses. Use words from the vocabulary box. Then, answer your partner's questions.

vocabulary box

greengrocer's
baker's
hairdresser's
butcher's
newsagent's
chemist's

James

Susan

Brian

Diane and Carl

Kelly and Kathy

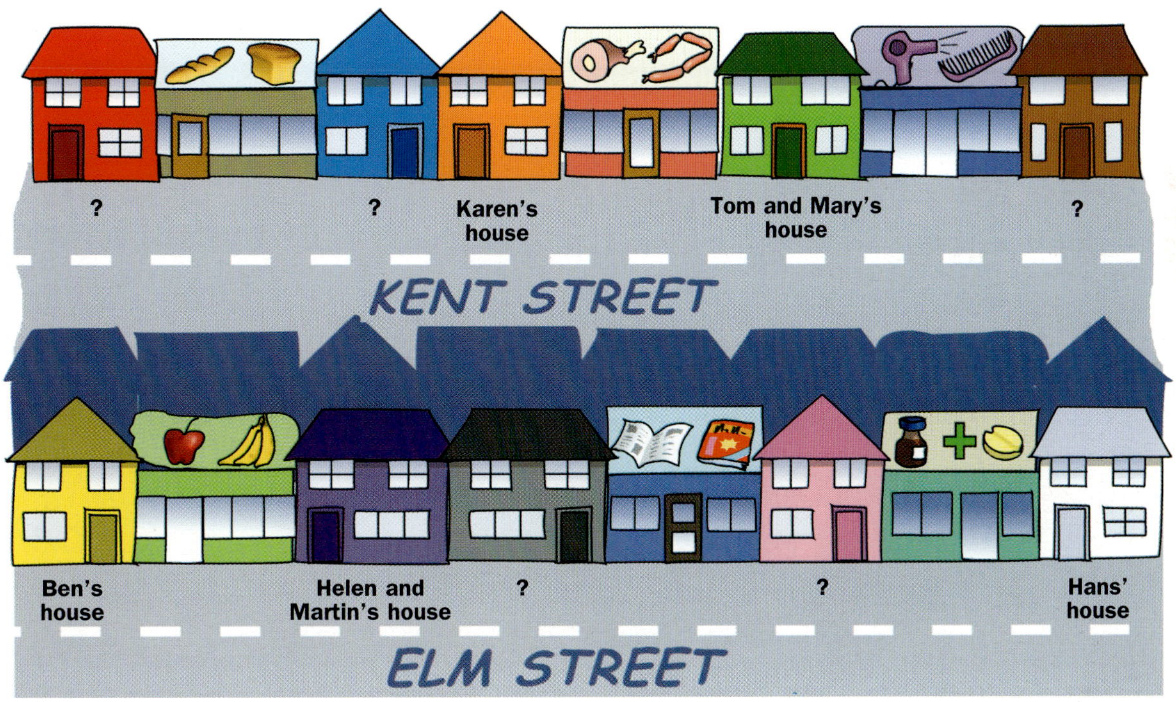

e.g. **A:** *What street do/does... live on?*
B: *He/She lives / They live on...*
A: *Is his/her/their house next to the...?*
B: *Yes, it is. / No, it isn't.*
A: *Is the red/blue house his/hers/theirs?*
B: *Yes, it is. / No, it isn't.*

Pairwork activities

STUDENT A

Unit 8

Look at the picture below and ask your partner questions, as in the example, to find out who the people are and who the animals belong to. Then, answer your partner's questions. Use words from the vocabulary box.

vocabulary box

take pictures
exercise
get on
get off
chase
cross

e.g. **A:** *Who's Robert?*
B: *He's the boy who/that...*
A: *Has he got a cat/dog?*
B: *Yes. The... which/that... is his. / No, he's got a... The... which/that... is his.*

Pairwork activities

STUDENT A

Unit 11

Tony and Lisa are organising a school dance which is taking place this Saturday. It is now Friday evening. Below is a list of things they must do before the dance. Look at the things Tony has done and ask your partner questions to find out what Lisa has done, as in the example. Then, answer your partner's questions. What haven't they done so far?

vocabulary box

advertise
hire
decorate
invite
put up

Things to do

- advertise in school paper ☐
- put up posters around school ☐
- buy food and drinks ☐
- hire a DJ to play music ☐
- clean gym ☐
- decorate gym ☐
- invite all the teachers ☐

Tony

Monday: advertise in school paper
Tuesday: clean gym
Friday: invite all the teachers

e.g. **A:** *Has Lisa put up posters around the school?*
B: *Yes, she has. She put up posters on... / No, she hasn't.*

Pairwork activities

STUDENT A

Unit 14

Look at the chart below. Ask your partner questions, as in the example, about what he/she likes doing or what he/she wants to do during his/her holiday and complete the chart. Then, look at the two hotel advertisements and suggest which hotel is the best for him/her. Then, complete the chart for yourself and answer your partner's questions. Which of the hotels your partner has got is the best for you?

e.g. **A:** *Do you like swimming?*
B: *Yes, I do. / No, I don't.*
A: *Do you want to go sightseeing during your holiday?*
B: *Yes, I do. / No, I don't.*

	Your partner	You
swim		
do sports		
dance		
try new things		
go shopping		
go sightseeing		
relax		
taste exotic food		

Gym

Lakeside restaurant

Area for horseback riding

We organise helicopter tours of the area

Swimming pool

Gym

Disco

Shopping centre

We organise tours of the city

Pairwork activities

STUDENT A

Unit 17

Happy Days International Summer Camp for Children is looking for a young person to work during the months of June, July and August. Two people have applied for the job. You have the information about Mark Newton and Student B has the information about Joe Stevens. Ask and answer questions to compare the information you have and decide which person is suitable for the job. Use question words.

Name:	Mark Newton	Joe Stevens
Age:	19	
Address:	6 Port Road (two miles from camp)	
Hobbies / Interests:	swimming, theatre	
Foreign languages:	Spanish, French	
Reasons for wanting this job:	likes working with children	
Can start work:	end of May	

e.g. **A:** *How old is Joe Stevens?*
B: *He's...*

Unit 19

Look at the picture of the woman and guess what she is / does / did / has done. Ask your partner for confirmation using question tags. Use ideas from the vocabulary box. Then, look at the picture and the information below and answer your partner's questions.

vocabulary box

actor	star in
director	direct
athlete	win medal
runner	do the long jump

- Mel Gibson
- comes from Australia
- actor / director
- starred in *Patriot / Mad Max / Lethal Weapon*
- directed *Braveheart*

?

e.g. **A:** *She's from... isn't she?*
B: *Yes, she is. / No, she isn't. She's from...*

Pairwork activities
STUDENT A

Unit 20

Look at the information in the boxes below and make correct sentences in the Passive Voice. Use the Present Simple Passive and the Past Simple Passive. Your partner will tell you if your sentences are correct. Then, listen to your partner, read the sentences in the orange box and tell him/her if his/her sentences are correct.

America	write	George Lucas
Television	discover	John Logie Baird
Star Wars	invent	Christopher Columbus
Romeo and Juliet	speak	Brazil
Portuguese	direct	William Shakespeare

e.g. **A:** *America was discovered by...*
B: *Correct! / Wrong, America was discovered by...*

- Australia was discovered by Captain James Cook.
- The radio was invented by Guglielmo Marconi.
- *Jurassic Park* was directed by Steven Spielberg.
- *Great Expectations* was written by Charles Dickens.
- English and French are spoken in Canada.

Pairwork activities

STUDENT A

Unit 21

Look at the notes about Tom Grisham's life. Some information is missing. Your partner has got the same notes but different information is missing. Ask him/her questions to complete the notes. Then, answer his/her questions. Use *before, after* and the *Past Perfect Simple*.

e.g. **B:** *What did Tom do after he had... ? / What had Tom done before he... ?*
A: *He...*

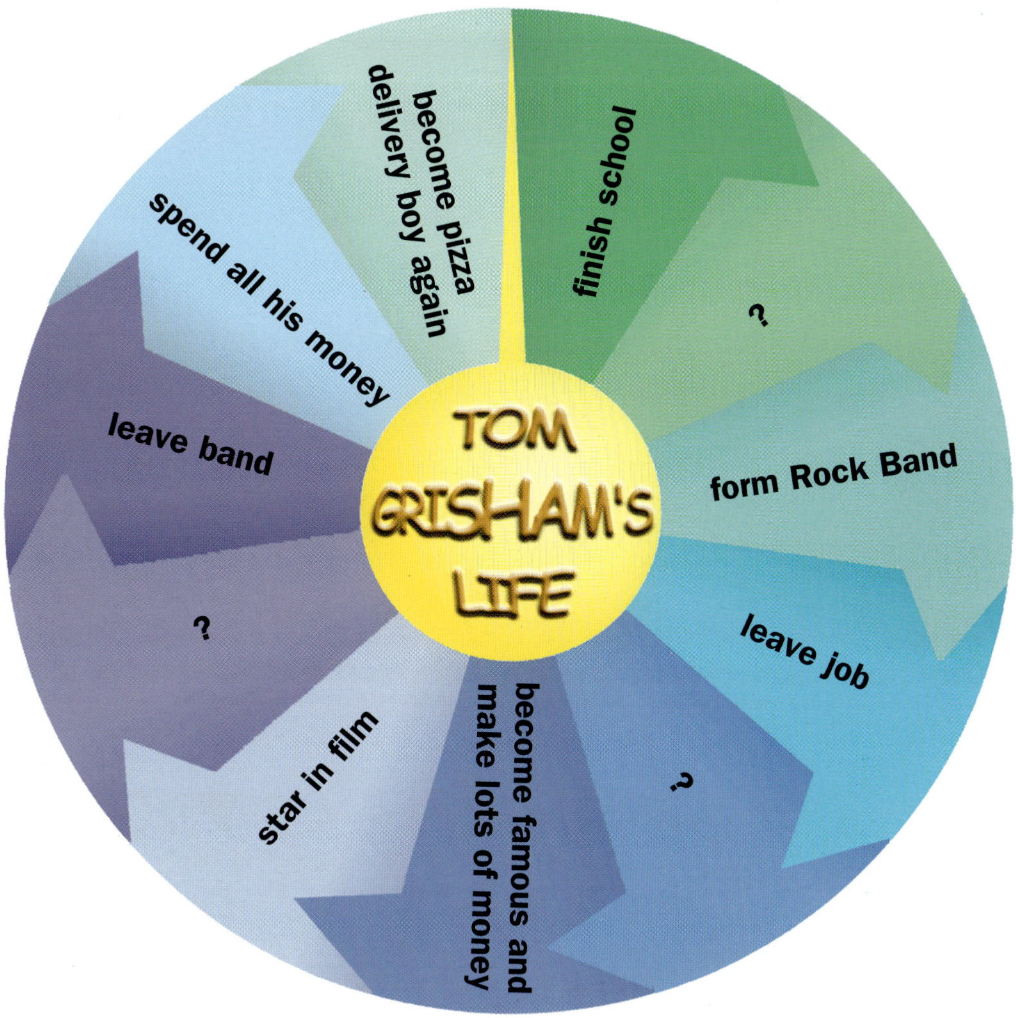

Pairwork activities

STUDENT B

Unit 1

The chart below shows what the Brown family usually do on Saturday morning and what they're doing today. Your partner has got the same chart, but different information is missing. Look at the chart and answer your partner's questions. Then, ask him/her questions to complete your chart. Use the ideas in the vocabulary box.

vocabulary box

watch cartoons
clean room
wash car
have coffee with friend
skate with friends
go on picnic
go shopping
work in garden

	Mrs Brown	Mr Brown	Tom	Betty and Judy
usually	?		?	
today		?		?

e.g. **B:** *Does Mrs Brown usually wash the car on Saturday morning?*
A: *Yes, she does. / No, she doesn't. She...*

Pairwork activities

STUDENT B

Unit 4

Who lives where? Look at the picture below and answer your partner's questions. Then, ask your partner questions to match the people with their houses. Use words from the vocabulary box.

vocabulary box

greengrocer's
baker's
hairdresser's
butcher's
newsagent's
chemist's

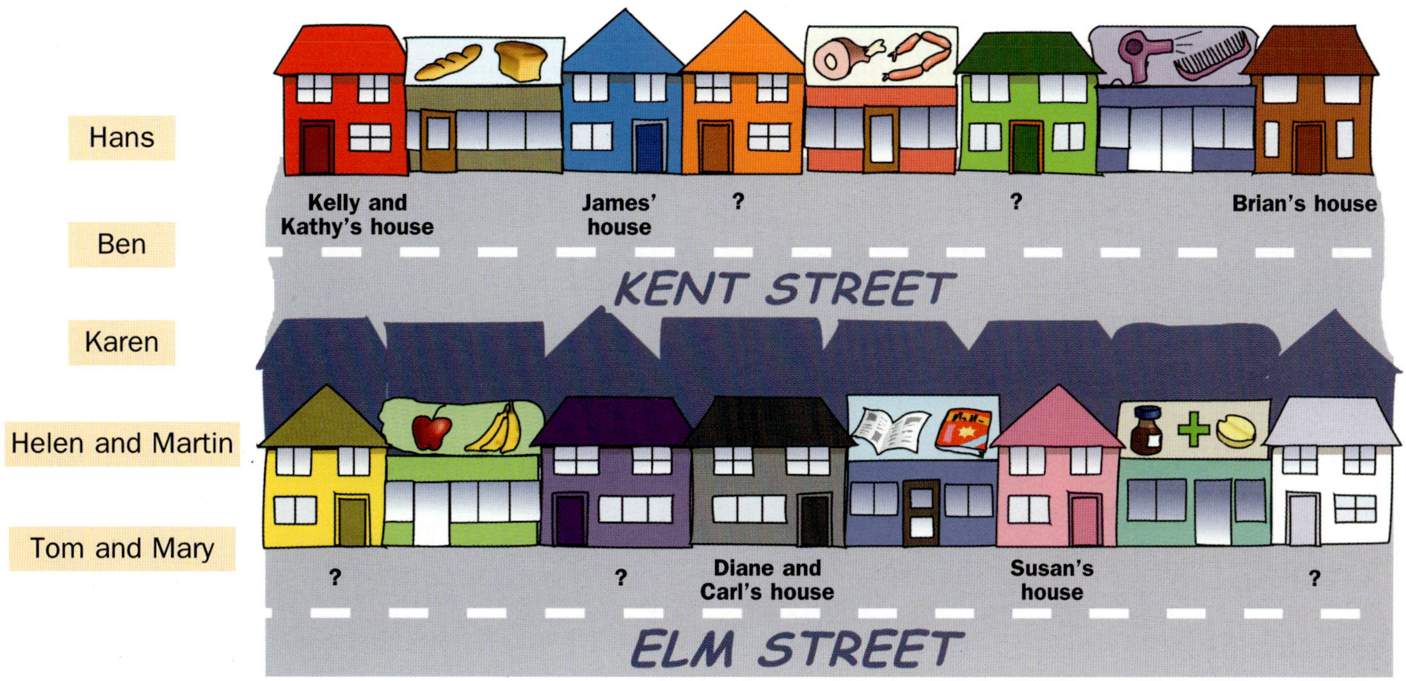

e.g. **B:** *What street do/does... live on?*
A: *He/She lives / They live on...*
B: *Is his/her/their house next to the...?*
A: *Yes, it is. / No, it isn't.*
B: *Is the red/blue house his/hers/theirs?*
A: *Yes, it is. / No, it isn't.*

Pairwork activities
STUDENT B

Unit 8

Look at the picture below and answer your partner's questions. Then, ask him/her questions, as in the example, to find out who the people are and who the animals belong to. Use words from the vocabulary box.

vocabulary box

take pictures
exercise
get on
get off
chase
cross

e.g. **B:** *Who's Cynthia?*
A: *She's the girl who/that...*
B: *Has she got a cat/dog?*
A: *Yes. The... which/that... is hers. / No, she's got a... The... which/that... is hers.*

Pairwork activities

STUDENT B

Unit 11

Tony and Lisa are organising a school dance which is taking place this Saturday. It is now Friday evening. Below is a list of things they must do before the dance. Look at the things Lisa has done and answer your partner's questions. Then, ask him/her questions, as in the example to find out what Tony has done. What haven't they done so far?

vocabulary box

advertise
hire
decorate
invite
put up

Things to do

- advertise in school paper
- put up posters around school
- buy food and drinks
- hire a DJ to play music
- clean gym
- decorate gym
- invite all the teachers

Lisa

Monday: put up posters around school
Wednesday: buy food and drinks
Thursday: hire a DJ to play music

e.g. **B:** *Has Tony advertised the dance in the school paper?*
A: *Yes, he has. He advertised it on... / No, he hasn't.*

Pairwork activities

STUDENT B

Unit 14

What do you like doing / want to do during a holiday? Complete the chart below for yourself and answer your partner's questions. Which of the hotels your partner has got is the best for you? Then, ask your partner questions, as in the example, about what he/she likes doing and what he/she wants to do during his/her holiday and complete the chart. Look at the two hotel advertisements and suggest which hotel is the best for him/her.

e.g. **B:** *Do you like swimming?*
A: *Yes, I do. / No, I don't.*
B: *Do you want to go sightseeing during your holiday?*
A: *Yes, I do. / No, I don't.*

	You	Your partner
swim		
do sports		
dance		
try new things		
go shopping		
go sightseeing		
relax		
taste exotic food		

Disco

Souvenir shop

We organise hiking trips

Swimming pool

Water sports

Disco

Caribbean restaurant

We organise island cruises

Pairwork activities

STUDENT B

Unit 17

Happy Days International Summer Camp for Children is looking for a young person to work during the months of June, July and August. Two people have applied for the job. You have the information about Joe Stevens and Student A has the information about Mark Newton. Ask and answer questions to compare the information you have and decide which person is suitable for the job. Use question words.

Name:	Joe Stevens	Mark Newton
Age:	19	
Address:	21 Milford Street (11 miles from camp)	
Hobbies / Interests:	sports cars, music	
Foreign languages:	French	
Reasons for wanting this job:	needs money to buy motorbike	
Can start work:	after June 15	

e.g. **B:** *How old is Mark Newton?*
A: *He's...*

Unit 19

Look at the picture and the information below and answer your partner's questions. Then, look at the picture of the man and guess what he is / does / did / has done. Ask your partner for confirmation using question tags. Use ideas from the vocabulary box.

vocabulary box

actor	star in
director	direct
athlete	win medal
runner	do the long jump

- Marion Jones
- comes from the USA
- athlete / runner
- runs 100m, 200m, 400m and does the long jump
- won gold medal (Olympics 2000)
- used to play basketball

?

e.g. **B:** *He's from... isn't he?*
A: *Yes, he is. / No, he isn't. He's from...*

Pairwork activities

STUDENT B

Unit 20

Listen to your partner, read the sentences in the orange box and tell him/her if his/her sentences are correct. Then, look at the prompts in the white boxes and make correct sentences in the Passive Voice. Use the Present Simple Passive and the Past Simple Passive. Your partner will tell you if your sentences are correct.

- America was discovered by Christopher Columbus.
- Television was invented by John Logie Baird.
- *Star Wars* was directed by George Lucas.
- *Romeo and Juliet* was written by William Shakespeare.
- Portuguese is spoken in Brazil.

Australia	write	Steven Spielberg
The radio	discover	Guglielmo Marconi
Jurassic Park	invent	Captain James Cook
Great Expectations	speak	Canada
English and French	direct	Charles Dickens

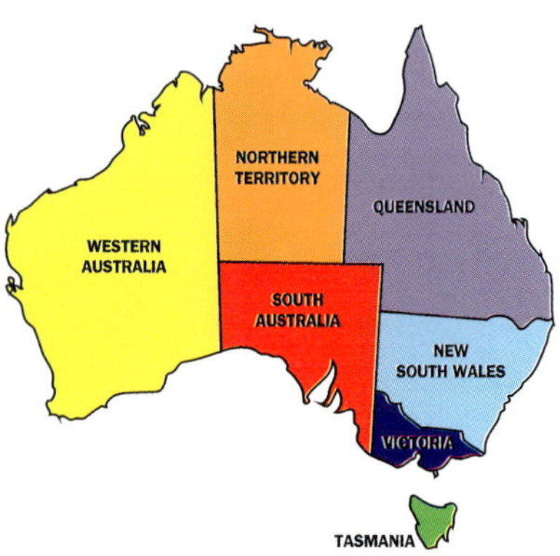

e.g. **B:** *Australia was discovered by...*
A: *Correct! / Wrong, Australia was discovered by...*

Pairwork activities
STUDENT B

Unit 21

Look at the notes about Tom Grisham's life. Some information is missing. Your partner has got the same notes but different information is missing. Answer his/her questions. Then, ask him/her questions to complete the notes. Use *before*, *after* and the *Past Perfect Simple*.

e.g. **B:** *What did Tom do after he had... ? / What had Tom done before he... ?*
A: *He...*

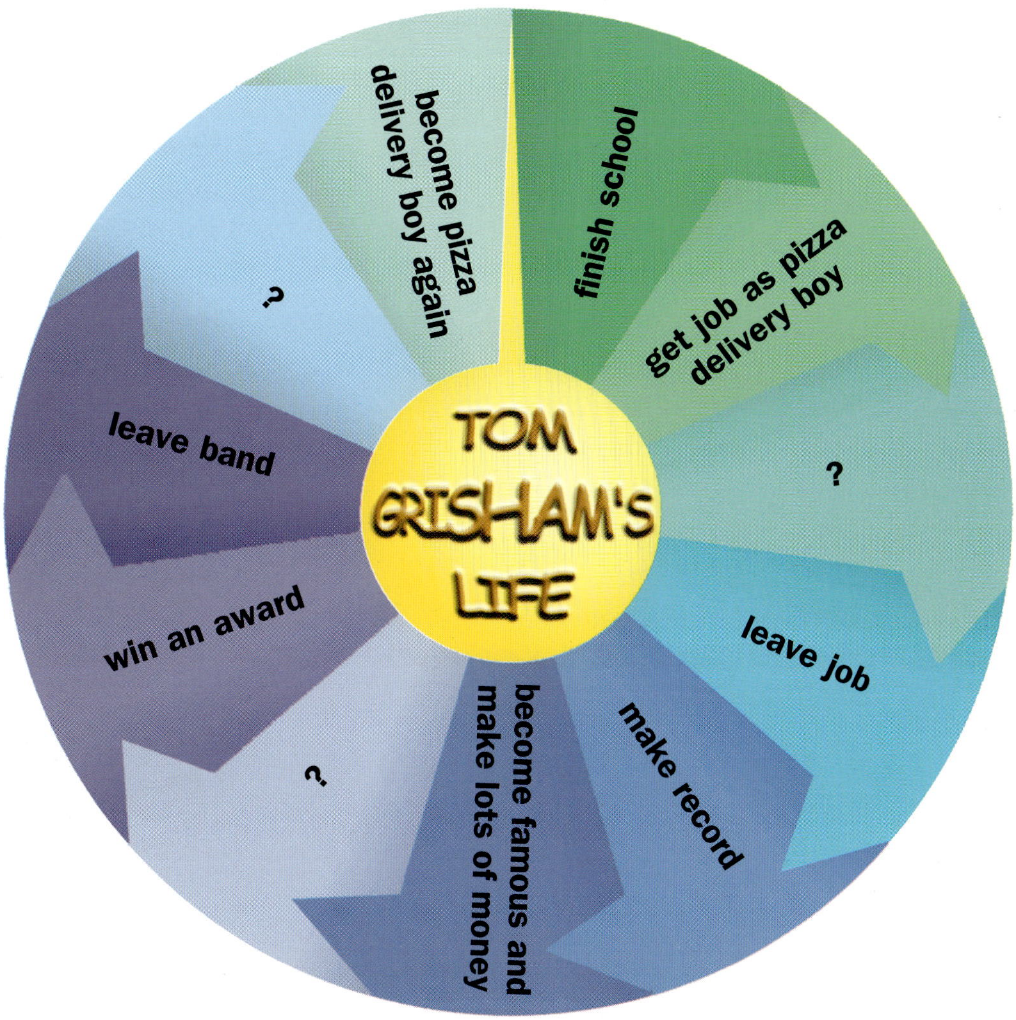

Irregular Verbs

Infinitive	Past	Past Participle
be	was / were	been
beat	beat	beaten
become	became	become
begin	began	begun
bite	bit	bitten
break	broke	broken
bring	brought	brought
build	built	built
burn	burnt	burnt
buy	bought	bought
catch	caught	caught
choose	chose	chosen
come	came	come
cost	cost	cost
cut	cut	cut
do	did	done
draw	drew	drawn
drink	drank	drunk
drive	drove	driven
eat	ate	eaten
fall	fell	fallen
feed	fed	fed
feel	felt	felt
fight	fought	fought
find	found	found
fly	flew	flown
forget	forgot	forgotten
freeze	froze	frozen
get	got	got
give	gave	given
go	went	gone
grow	grew	grown
have	had	had
hear	heard	heard
hide	hid	hidden
hit	hit	hit
hold	held	held
hurt	hurt	hurt
keep	kept	kept
know	knew	known

Irregular Verbs

Infinitive	Past	Past Participle
learn	learnt	learnt
leave	left	left
lend	lent	lent
let	let	let
lie	lay	lain
lose	lost	lost
make	made	made
meet	met	met
pay	paid	paid
put	put	put
read	read	read
ride	rode	ridden
ring	rang	rung
rise	rose	risen
run	ran	run
say	said	said
see	saw	seen
sell	sold	sold
send	sent	sent
shine	shone	shone
show	showed	shown
sing	sang	sung
sit	sat	sat
sleep	slept	slept
speak	spoke	spoken
spend	spent	spent
stand	stood	stood
steal	stole	stolen
swim	swam	swum
take	took	taken
teach	taught	taught
tell	told	told
think	thought	thought
throw	threw	thrown
understand	understood	understood
wake	woke	woken
wear	wore	worn
win	won	won
write	wrote	written

Word List

A
a bit
abroad
accident
address
adult
advertise
advice
advise
aerobics
aeroplane
ago
agree
ahead of
all night long
almost
a long time ago
amazing
ambulance
amusement park
ancient
angry
appear
archaeologist
area
Argentina
around
arrive
article
artist
assistant
astronaut
athlete
award
away
awful

B
back
badminton
baker
baker's
band
bank robber
bar (of chocolate)
barbecue
bark
bath
be afraid of
be interested in
beat
bee
beginning
believe
belly
below
best seller
billion
biology
bite
board game
bookshop
boring
borrow
boss
both
bowl
break (n)
bridge
brush (n)
brush (v)
build
building
bungee-jumping
burn
businessman
bus stop
butcher's

C
cabin
café
call
camp (v)
camp (n)
campsite
canary
candle
canoe
can't stand
canyon
capital city
captain
care
car park
carton
cartoon
castle
catch
cathedral
cave
celebrate
celebration
centre
century
certainly
certificate
change
changing room
chase
check
cheetah
chemistry
chemist's
chess
choose
circus
classmate
cliff
clothes
clown
club
coin
cold (n)
collect
comedy
come from

comfortable
comic book
competition
concert
concert hall
connect
continent
continue
control
cook (n)
corner
cornflakes
correct
cost (v)
country
couple
cousin
crash
creature
cricket
cross
crowded
cruise
cry

D

damage (v)
dance
dangerous
dark
daughter
decide
decorate
deep
deer
delicious
dentist
desert
diary
dictionary
die
different
difficult
difficulty
dining hall
dining room
dinosaur
direct
disappear
disco
discover
dish
display
dive
diver
diving
DJ
documentary
dog-house
dolphin
don't mind
doorbell
dream
drummer
during

E

earn
earth
Easter
Egypt
electric
electrician
else
e-mail
end
engine
enjoy
enter
entry
environment
equipment
especially
eucalyptus
exactly
except
excited
exciting
exercise (v)
exit
exotic
explain
explore

F

factory
fall asleep
famous
fast food restaurant
favourite
feed
feel
female
fence
fight
finally
fine
finger
Finland
fireworks
first
first aid kit
fish (v)
fit
fix
flight
following
footprint
foreign
forever
fork
form (v)
fortunately
free
free time
freeze
frog
front
funny
future

G

gallery
garage
gentleman
get off
get on
get up

ghost
giraffe
give sb a bath
glass
glove
goal
go camping
go on a diet
go on a safari
go out
go sightseeing
gold
goldfish
goose
grammar
grass
greengrocer's
group
grow
guess
guest
gym

H

hairdresser's
handwriting
hang-gliding
happen
hate
have a great time
have fun
head
headache
health
healthy
heavily
heavy
helicopter
helmet
hide
high
High School
hiking
hill
hire
hit
hobby
hockey
hold
hope
horrible
horseback riding
however
huge
hungry
hunt
hurry
hurt
husband

I

ice
ice-skating
idea
igloo
ill
immediately
important
improve
increase
India
indoor
injure
insect
interest (n)
interesting
in the middle of
invent
invite
Ireland
Irish
iron (v)
ironing
island

J

jacket
jigsaw puzzle
job
jogging
join
jump
jungle
junk food
just

K

kangaroo
keep
kill
kilometre
kind
knee
knowledge

L

lake
land
language
later
laugh
lazy
leaf
learner
leave
lemonade
lend
let
library
lie
lie
lift
light (adj)
light (n)
line
list
litre
live
loaf
local
lock
long jump
look for
look like
look out
lose
lottery
loud

loudly
luckily
lucky

M

machine
magazine
main
make sure
manage
map
marry
Mars
marsupial
match
Mathematics
maybe
meal
mean (v)
medal
member
menu
midnight
mile
million
mirror
Miss
miss
mobile phone
model
model plane
modern
moment
monkey
monster
moon
motorbike
mountain range
move
museum
musical instrument
musician

N

name (v)
Natural History
need
neighbour
neighbourhood
Netherlands
news
newsagent's
newspaper
New Year's Eve
noise
noisy
north
Norway
nowadays
nurse

O

ocean
offer (v)
office
on business
on my own
on time
once
orange juice
orchestra
order (v)
organise
other
outside
oven
own
owner

P

pack
packet
paint
painting
paper
park (v)
parrot
pass
passport
past
patiently
pay
pay attention
penguin
perhaps
person
pet
petrol
phone (v)
photographer
photography
picnic
piece
pill
pilot
place
plan (n)
plane
planet
plant (v)
plant (n)
plate
player
playground
pleased
pocket
poem
Poland
polar bear
police
police car
police officer
police station
polite
polluted
poor
post office
practice
practise
prefer
prepare
present (n)
president
prison
probably
project
promise (v)
protect

pub
publish
puppy
put on
put up
puzzle
pyramid

Q

question
quick
quiet
quite

R

race
radio
railway station
rain (v)
reach
reading
ready
real
really
reason
record (n)
recycle
relax
remember
repair
reptile
return
rice
ride (n)
ride (v)
right now
ring (n)
ring (v)
rise
river
road
rock
roof
round
ruin
rule
runner
rush (n)

S

safety
sausage
Scandinavia
scare
scared
science fiction
scientist
score (v)
scream (v)
second-hand
secret (n)
seem
sell
send
several
sheep
shelf
shop
shopping centre
shout
show (v)
shower
shy
sign
singer
skate
ski (v)
skier
skirt
skis (n)
sleep (n)
sleeping bag
slice
slow
smell
smile (v)
smoke
snack
snow (n)
snow (v)
sofa
soft drink
soldier
son
south
South Pole
souvenir
space
space travel
spend
spend time
spider
spoon
sports centre
square
squash
stage
stairs
stamp
star in
station
stay
steal
still
stone age
straight
street
stressed
strong
studio
study
subject
suddenly
suggest
suitcase
sunbathe
sunglasses
surprised
survey
Sweden
sweet
sweet shop
swimming pool
Switzerland

T

table tennis
take care of

take off
take part in
take place
taste (v)
teach
team
telephone (n)
tent
terrible
terribly
Thailand
then
think
throw
ticket
tidy (v)
time
tinned food
together
toothache
top
torch
touch
tour
tour guide
tourist
towards
town hall
traditional
traffic
train (v)
trainers
treehouse
trip
trouble
true
try
try on
try out
tunnel
turn
turn off
turn on
twice
twin

U

unhappy
uniform
university
unless
until
use (v)
useful

V

van
vegetables
village
voice

W

walk (n)
wallet
war
warm
washing-up
water-polo
waterfall
water sports
way
weak
weather
weekday
weight
welcome
west
wet
wet suit
whale
while
wide
wife
wild
win
without
wonderful
wood
work (v)
world
worry
writer
wrong

Live English Grammar Elementary
Student's Book
H.Q. Mitchell - S. Parker

Published by: **MM Publications**
www.mmpi.net www.mmpi.co.uk
info@mmpi.net

Offices
Great Britain - Greece - Poland - France - Cyprus
Associated companies and representatives throughout the world.

ISBN for the International edition: 960-379-425-2
ISBN for the MM Publications German edition: 960-379-916-5

ISBN for the MM Publications - Langenscheidt edition: 3-526-51706-1